The New American VEGETARIAN M·E·N·U COOKBOOK

The New American
VEGETARIAN
M·E·N·U
COOKBOOK
From Everyday Dining to Elegant Entertaining

Paulette Mitchell

RODALE PRESS
Emmaus, Pennsylvania

Edited by	Carol Munson
Copy edited by	Charles Bell
	Russell Meyer
Cover design by	Linda Jacopetti
Cover photograph by	Mitchell T. Mandel
Design and Layout by	The Bookmakers, Incorporated
Illustrations by	Diane Ness Shaw
Recipe testing by	Anita Hirsch
	JoAnn Coponi
	Rhonda Diehl

Copyright © 1984 by Paulette Mitchell

Library of Congress Cataloging in Publication Data

Mitchell, Paulette.
  The new American vegetarian menu cookbook.

  Includes index.
  1. Vegetarian cookery. 2. Cookery, American.
I. Title.
TX837.M65   1984   641.5′636   83-24703
ISBN 0-87857-501-4 hardcover
ISBN 0-87857-494-8 paperback

  6 8 10 9 7   hardcover

4 6 8 10 9 7 5 3   paperback

To my husband, John,
whose love inspired my cooking
and whose encouragement inspired this book

Contents

MENUS AND RECIPES

INTRODUCING VEGETARIANISM

Vegetarianism: A New Cuisine

One evening, while dining in a favorite vegetarian restaurant, my husband and I discussed the idea of eating meatless meals all the time. We decided, right then, to try it as an experiment. That was more than eight years ago. We never had any desire to go back to our old eating habits. It's been fun both seeking out vegetarian and natural foods restaurants to test their specialties and trying the surprising variety of meatless entrees offered in traditional restaurants. Best of all, entertaining has taken on an added pleasure because it gives us a chance to share favorite vegetarian dishes with our friends — who all seem to enjoy eating at our house.

My passion for cooking actually began with the change to vegetarian eating. With meat out of our diet, it became necessary to experiment with new foods and to combine familiar ones in new ways. As it turned out, the challenge of presenting those foods in attractive, tasty, well-balanced meals was truly enjoyable. It still is.

After our vegetarian eating pattern was established, my husband and I decided to go a step further and eliminate refined sweeteners, white flour, excessive sodium, and processed foods from our diet. With these modifications I realized that some of my favorite recipes now needed a new approach to flavorings and garnishes.

As part of my search for fresh ideas, I not only studied the basics of vegetarian and natural foods cooking but also explored the mysteries of classical and ethnic cuisines. From my travels in this country and abroad, I picked up ideas for ethnic menus and unusual food presentations. All this information enabled me to create hundreds of new recipes, many for this book, as well as some that are especially appropriate as demonstrations in the cooking classes I conduct.

My experience with a vegetarian diet has been rewarding. I am particularly gratified to see my husband, who grew up eating meat every day, thoroughly enjoying the variety of flavors and textures in the meat-free meals I prepare and finding them satisfying. Personally, I feel healthy and energetic on a diet that contains no meat, and I can easily maintain the same weight level and figure that I had when I was a model. Best of all, after going through a normal pregnancy while maintaining my basic vegetarian diet, I recently gave birth to a healthy, strong boy.

The vegetarian experience has been happy and positive for my family in every way. I hope you will find the same pleasure, satisfaction, and good health when you begin eating meals without meat.

EXCITEMENT IN A NEW CUISINE

I see an exciting new cuisine evolving from vegetarian and natural foods cooking. This cuisine is light, lean, and fresh — just what we want to emphasize these days. My recipes reflect this by featuring an abundance of refreshing fruits and vegetables, as well as whole grains and beans, which are both satisfying and low in fat. Nuts, seeds, cheese, and eggs are flavorful but high in calories, so I use them prudently. The dishes are enhanced with herb seasonings — not with salt. For desserts, I use only unrefined sweetners.

Of course, just about any recipe works best with fresh ingredients because their original flavor and texture is undiminished by processing. For that reason, I avoid frozen or canned products. Dishes made with fresh ingredients look better too.

It takes some practice to plan a successful, nutritionally balanced menu based on an unfamiliar cuisine, such as vegetarian cooking might be to you. To help novices over this hurdle, I have organized my recipes into menus, but at best these menus only suggest the wide range of possibilities for creating meatless meals. You will also find that the dishes, many of which can be made quickly or made in advance, call for ingredients that are readily available. In addition, the menu plans reflect my belief that mealtime should be special. It's true that we sometimes need to rush, but the real appreciation of food comes when we take time to savor it and to relax in the company of those dining with us.

Vegetarian cuisine is exciting in its own right; it is not merely a substitute for cuisines that include meat. For many people, a flavorful pasta and cheese dish or a vegetable soufflé is a clear choice over one with meat, even though they may not be vegetarians. Personally I enjoy this way of eating simply because it offers so much good taste and eye appeal and because it is so satisfying and healthful.

NUTRITION IN A VEGETARIAN CUISINE

Individuals, especially pregnant women and children, who choose a vegetarian diet must cultivate an awareness of the daily need for complete protein. For those who eat meat, complete protein is almost automatic, but vegetarians must plan for it. Excellent nonmeat sources of protein include eggs, cheese, milk, milk products, nuts, seeds, whole grains, dry beans, and lentils.

Protein is made up of twenty-two different amino acids, all necessary to good health. Although the body produces fourteen of these amino acids on its own, the other eight (called essential amino acids) must come from the foods we eat. All the essential amino acids must be present simultaneously and in specific proportions, if our bodies are to make efficient use of the protein we consume. Meats are considered *complete* proteins because they contain all eight essential amino acids. Such foods as nuts, legumes, and grains are *incomplete* proteins because they do not individually contain all the amino acids.

By combining some foods that are deficient in certain amino acids with other foods that have them, you can easily make sure that you are consuming complete protein. For example, legumes are deficient in two of the amino acids that are plentiful in grains. When you eat both foods at the same meal, your body receives complete protein. The peasant cultures of many nations commonly take advantage of this principle when they combine bean or pea dishes with rice, bread, tortillas, or some other grain food. A dairy product paired with nuts and seeds is another excellent combination that adds up to a complete protein. The Nutloaf recipe in this book provides an example of such a combination — cottage cheese with cashews, walnuts, pecans, and sunflower seeds. Naturally, eating a variety of whole foods also helps to ensure an adequate intake of complete proteins and other nutrients. You will find this kind of diversity in the menus.

SHOPPING FOR WHOLE FOODS

Check the labels for additives when you buy packaged foods. Almost all of them contain additives — some to improve appearance, others to improve shelf life. Few can improve on the food values of the original, so I avoid them. Reading labels is especially important for strict vegetarians because animal products like gelatin often appear in the most unlikely items. When I buy fresh ingredients and prepare them myself, I know exactly what each dish contains. More than that, I've had the pleasure of preparing them myself.

Because I look for unprocessed foods, I do most of my shopping in the outer perimeter of the grocery store — where the fruits, vegetables, and dairy products are usually found. I avoid the inner aisles where packaged foods are stocked. Whenever I can, I buy high quality produce at seasonal fruit and vegetable markets, and food co-ops are my source for reasonably priced staples like beans, nuts, flours, and grains. However, the ingredients used in the recipes for this book are available in most supermarkets.

Whether shopping in a supermarket or elsewhere, my food expenses are often less than they were when I prepared dishes containing meat. When the week's menu contains several rice and bean dishes, my food expenditures are the lowest, yet the meals are satisfying and very tasty.

EFFICIENCY IN THE KITCHEN

In my cooking classes, one of my students invariably brings up the idea that vegetarian cooking must take more time than cooking with meat. It doesn't. Good vegetarian cuisine, like any other good cuisine, that doesn't call for processed or packaged convenience foods, offers a number of quick and easy dishes. Each section of this book contains recipes that can be prepared in a short time.

I love to cook and entertain, but I also love the busy and active life I lead outside my home. The key to managing both well is planning. Here are some procedures that help me both when I plan everyday meals and when I gear up for entertaining.

Plan menus for a week at a time. I write them down and post them inside a cabinet door. With a calendar handy, I can then select quick, easy menus for busy days and save the more elaborate ones for days when I can spend extra time in the kitchen.

By consulting the meal plans, I am also certain to use leftovers and fresh foods before they spoil and to ensure that my meals check out in terms of nutritional content and balance. If I'm going to entertain, the plan helps me to decide on the method of serving, the serving pieces I want to use, and the table setting. I also jot down reminders about advance preparations that can be made when time permits.

With a week's menus in hand, I can make a reliable grocery list. I check each recipe for ingredients to see which I have on hand and which must be bought. In the corner of the menu, I also list staple items such as flour or oils as they run low and add these to the list. (Is anything more frustrating than having to run to the store in the middle of a cooking spree?) To cut down on shopping time, I even list items in an order that matches the sections of the store where I generally buy my food. Unless I see a terrific special in the store, I rarely alter my menu plan or purchase items that are not on my list.

In the chapter "Back to Basics" I provide recipes for such items as Mayonnaise and Mustard. Rather than prepare these recipes as needed, you can make them as I do, when time permits and keep a supply on hand.

My recipe notes are other useful tools. After preparing a dish, I jot notes on the recipe as a reminder of any changes I made in the recipe or changes I would like to make next time I serve the dish. If vegetarian and natural foods cooking are new to you, however, it is wise to be cautious about making such changes. Better to start with recipes designed for cooking this way.

Two notebooks play a special role in my kitchen. In one I keep lists of successful recipes, divided into such categories as appetizers, main dishes, vegetables, or desserts. Every time I try a new recipe, I enter it in the appropriate section, with the book and page (or the section in my recipe file) where it can be found. Recipes that have proved popular with me and my family or guests are starred.

In the second notebook, I record my successful menus. (Great menus are a work of art and deserve to be repeated — in fact, this cookbook actually began with that very menu record book.) It is a timesaving guide for weekly menu planning and entertaining. I note guests to whom each menu has been served, which menus are quick and easy favorites for busy days, and which parts of a menu work well when an abbreviated menu is needed.

Like most avid cooks I am a perpetual recipe clipper. For easy access to such recipes, I file them in a letter-size file box organized by recipe categories. Each week, I try to include at least one or two of these new recipes in my menus. Admittedly, I'll probably never live long enough to try them all.

When you get down to the actual cooking, you need what you need when you need it. I store utensils in the part of the kitchen where they are used and keep the items I use frequently within easy reach. Kitchen equipment does not need to be elaborate, but I think a food processor is well worth its price. It saves a considerable amount of time and effort, particularly when a recipe calls for chopped vegetables or nuts. Other utensils that are indispensible to me include a set of sharp knives, a vegetable steamer, a variety of mixing bowls, and a good set of pots and pans. Owning a multitude of gadgets is fun but not essential. (On the other hand, what would I do without my parsley washer?)

TIPS ON QUICK MEALS

Long preparation time is not always necessary to produce an excellent meal. In fact, most of the recipes in this book can be prepared quickly with minimum effort. The secret is simplicity.

The menus in each section are arranged in a progression from easy, quick preparations to more complex ones that require additional time. Several of the menus, particularly in the "Feasts and Buffets" section, are lengthy, but they are made up of relatively short individual recipes. When your cooking time is limited and you can make only part of the menu, just take care to retain the protein dish. If you eliminate an appetizer or side dish, the courses that remain will be ample.

I rarely do all the cooking for a meal at one time. When preparing to entertain, you can often begin the main course one or two days ahead, making the salad, dessert, and garnishes on the day of the party. With sensible timing, none of the menu components will require freezing and none will deteriorate. Such early preparation allows you more time to consider added touches and helps you to feel more relaxed for your party.

As an example, consider the first menu on page 145 in the "Elegant Dinners" section. Two days before the get-together, I would prepare, cover, and refrigerate the salad dressing, the rice, and the muffins. The next day, I would begin making the Orange Carrot Soup and stop just before the half-and-half is to be added. I would also steam and refrigerate the vegetables and make the pie crust. Early on the day of the party, I would assemble the casserole, make the pie filling, and fill the crust. Shortly before the guests arrive, I would assemble the salad ingredients. Then, when it was almost time to serve the dinner, I would heat and complete the soup, toss the salad, warm the muffins, reheat the casserole, and garnish the pie. These last few procedures can be done quickly just prior to serving each course. In this way, you can enjoy the dinner yourself.

On days when my time for cooking is limited, I generally use leftovers. Two of my favorite ways of using these are as omelet fillings or over a baked potato. Quick Cashew Creole is delicious spooned over a baked potato; Garden Vegetable Stir-Fry makes a delightful omelet filling; Ratatouille is tasty presented either way. Always serve leftovers with the same care that went into their initial creation, and no one will ever know they're eating a short-cut dinner.

VEGETARIAN MENUS FOR ENTERTAINING

Planning a vegetarian menu for guests who eat meat seems like a challenge at first. But just remind yourself that everyone likes good food, so if you serve truly tasty dishes, you are bound to get a favorable reaction.

Traditional ethnic dishes that are also meatless are usually good, safe choices when you are not familiar with your guests' tastes. Sometimes serving a menu that has some exotic elements actually enhances the success of the meal. Once your reputation as a good cook is established, you can serve almost any kind of dish with confidence. Friends approach our vegetarian dinner parties eagerly, and they leave happy and stimulated by what's been served and looking forward to next time.

Whether it is a party or a family meal, I take the manner of service very seriously. Sometimes I serve several dishes at once; other times I serve the courses in series. One disadvantage of putting the whole meal on the table at once is that everyone tends to rush through it. Better to savor separate courses. A dinner served that way is no more difficult to prepare than one served all at once. The presentation is often preferable because it allows you to set out the dishes at the optimum serving temperature.

MENU PLANNING

You may follow the menus of this book just as they are or split them to create new ones. The same is true for the menus and recipes suggested in separate chapters. For example, many brunch recipes and menus adapt well to lunches or suppers.

I am guided by many considerations in menu planning. Here are several that might serve as helpful guidelines for you. Think of a good menu as a good story — with the proper balance of dramatic elements. The requirements are the same regardless of whether or not the meal includes meat.

Try for a variety of foods with a range of nutrients in each meal, being sure to include at least one protein-rich food in every menu, and learn to combine foods to form complete protein. You needn't plan a menu around one course; after all, appetizers and desserts also play a part in balancing the nutrients. A fine meatless meal can consist of two or three complementary courses of equal importance, or you might prefer to focus on a star course, not necessarily the main course. We all know that birthday cake can be the highlight of a meal!

To stimulate interest, vary colors within a menu. Imagine yellow squash, carrots, and cornbread in the same meal — what a boring picture! Use brightly colored garnishes to offset bland-colored foods, like the green of watercress or parsley to complement brown rice. Avoid using a food more than once in a meal (even if your tomatoes are ripe and abundant), and don't plan a meal consisting entirely of vegetables.

The varied intensity of flavors contributes a great deal to the success of a menu. Take advantage of this by surrounding the entree with dishes that complement it rather than do battle. I generally serve only one highly spiced course in a meal. The same need for sensitivity applies in using sweet and tart flavors.

Creamy or soft textures are balanced by the crunchy raw or lightly cooked vegetables and crunchy nuts or seeds. It's seldom appropriate to serve more than one course with a sauce, or cream, or eggs. Think of the monotony of a meal that includes a cream soup, a sauced main dish, and baked custard for dessert. If sauces are to be used in any other course, then a light oil-type is my choice for the salad dressing instead of a mayonnaise-based one.

For fun I like to end a light meal with a really luscious dessert. But that's too much after a heavy dinner, so I often use fruit or sherbet as a finish then.

From a visual point of view, ingredients chopped into the same relative sizes look the most pleasing. Best of all, similarly sized pieces of food tend to cook at the same rate, and that enhances the appearance and texture of the finished dish. I apply this basic principle of oriental cooking to many dishes.

Take the season of the year and the weather into account when planning what to serve. Make the most of fresh, seasonal foods — that way you use high quality ingredients that can also provide a focus for a menu. November's crisp weather certainly dictates a menu that's different from one for a picnic in August. In summer, an all-chilled menu can be refreshing, but a single heated dish will add variety to your meal.

The flair and showmanship of a creative cook are released when a special dining event offers the opportunity. Holiday themes or those related to some reason for celebration often guide me in recipe selection as well as table trimmings and appropriate house decorations. I believe these personal touches make my family and guests feel they are important.

You must try to take into account the food preferences of your guests and any dietary restrictions, if you are aware of them. If I am having a luncheon attended by women, I will serve food lower in calories food than I might for a weekend or holiday party that includes both women and men. Also, I try to anticipate hunger levels at the time of day we will be eating.

Sometimes, a touch of the unexpected raises the appeal of everyday cooking, and it certainly pleases guests. Be innovative — serve the meal in an unusual setting or perk up the dishes with striking garnishes such as a bit of cranberry relish in a pocket of mashed sweet potatoes or popcorn on cheese soup. Sometimes I deliberately serve an out-of-season surprise (if the quality is good) such as fresh strawberries in mid-December.

The number of dishes you can prepare, their complexity, and the number of guests you can serve comfortably depend to a great extent on the kind of kitchen you have. For example, unless you have two ovens, you soon learn not to use menus that require cooking two dishes at different temperatures. I have carefully avoided such situations with the menus presented here.

Take stock of your available time when making your plans. Overwork and a frenzied atmosphere can ruin a pleasant event for the cook. My main goals are to enjoy my own parties and to make my guests feel comfortable.

Finally, as you plan each menu, consider how to serve the meal. Select the appointments — the table linens, dishes, flowers, and candles — that set the scene, and the garnishes and attractively arranged platters that will dress up the food. Try for elegant simplicity, just enough touches to make the occasion and the food special.

Let your heart and instinct run free; be happy and relaxed in the kitchen, and have fun!

A Word about Ingredients

The ingredients used in preparing the recipes in this book are generally available in supermarkets. Some of them may be displayed in specialty areas, however, such as Oriental foods, Middle Eastern foods, or natural foods sections. If these items are unfamiliar to you, the following section provides information on the natural and ethnic foods called for in many of the recipes. It also describes how to make some foods, such as yogurt, that can easily and inexpensively be prepared in your own kitchen.

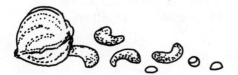

BRAN

Bran is the outside layer which protects a grain until the kernel is planted. When the grain is milled to create a refined flour, the bran is removed. For this reason, refined flours have less fiber than whole grain flours.

To increase the fiber content of recipes, I often add bran to cereals and to such baked goods as cookies and muffins. The bran used in recipes in this book is wheat bran, which is high in fiber and contains several of the minerals and vitamins (especially the B vitamins) in wheat.

Bran keeps well if stored in an airtight container. It tends not to become rancid because it is fairly low in fat.

BROWN RICE

Brown rice is the whole rice kernel from which only the hull has been removed during processing. Because the bran is left on, brown rice is higher in fiber, vitamins, and minerals than white rice. It's a source of nonmeat protein that is nicely complemented by dry beans, dairy products, and seeds. Long grain brown rice separates more easily after cooking than short or medium grain varieties, and thus tends to be fluffier.

Cook rice by simmering in water or stock. Use twice as much liquid as rice. Bring the rice and liquid to a boil, cover, reduce heat to low, and simmer gently until the water is absorbed, 35 to 45 minutes. Do not stir rice during the cooking period. Stirring encourages rice to become sticky and gummy.

Store raw brown rice in a tightly covered container in a cool, dry place. Cooked rice will keep for several days in the refrigerator or for a month in the freezer.

BULGUR AND CRACKED WHEAT

Bulgur, a nutritious, easily prepared grain, is a form of processed wheat with an appealing nutty flavor. Bulgur is made by boiling wheat kernels, drying them, removing the bran and cracking the kernels. Its nutrients—protein and B vitamins—are the same as those in whole wheat, but in slightly smaller quantities.

Because bulgur is pre-cooked and dried, the kernels may be stored satisfactorily for much longer periods than regular wheat. Like most grains, however, it should be stored in a cool, dry place in a bug-proof and airtight container.

Cook bulgur in water or stock; add the liquid to 1½ or 2 times the amount of grain. Cover, and simmer about 10 minutes. Or, reconstitute bulgur by placing it in a shallow pan and pouring boiling water over it to a height of ½ inch above the bulgur. Let stand until the water is absorbed, about 30 minutes. Soaked bulgur will keep, covered, up to a week in the refrigerator.

Cracked wheat and bulgur are interchangeable in many recipes, although they are not identical. Both are whole grain wheats which have been cracked, but bulgur has been parboiled and then dried, whereas cracked wheat has not been cooked and, thus, using it requires more preparation.

Used in such recipes as Tabbouleh, bulgur is popular throughout the eastern Mediterranean and the Middle East.

CAROB (CAROB FLOUR, ST. JOHN'S BREAD)

Carob is the ground dried fruit of the carob tree, grown mostly in the Mediterranean region and the Middle East. Because products made from carob often resemble chocolate, some people consider the fruit a chocolate substitute. Carob doesn't taste as rich as chocolate, but it has its own unique flavor.

Consider carob for its own merits. Unlike chocolate and cocoa, carob has little fat, few calories, and no caffeine. It is naturally sweet, and contains fiber, calcium, phosphorus, and potassium.

Carob is available in several forms: powder, carob chips, blocks of carob for baking or cooking, and powdered carob mixes for making a hot carob beverage. Because some of these forms often contain brown sugar, read the package label to be aware of the ingredients you are using.

Carob powder is less soluble than cocoa, so a gritty sediment often remains in beverages. For a better consistency, heat a smooth paste of carob and water before adding it to the other ingredients, or prepare the beverage in a blender.

Carob powder will keep up to a year in a closed container in a dry place. Sometimes, excess moisture will cause lumps to form in carob powder. If this happens, break the lumps in a separate bowl before adding the powder to your recipe.

COUSCOUS

Couscous is a wheat product made by forming tiny pellets from a mixture of flour and water. It is best known for its use in the traditional North African dish of the same name. It can be purchased in supermarkets or natural foods stores. It should be stored in a tightly covered jar on your pantry shelf.

DRIED BEANS (LEGUMES)

Beans are seeds: embryonic plants containing enough nourishment for the first stages of growth. Though the various legumes differ slightly in their nutritional value, all are good sources of vegetable protein, carbohydrates, several B vitamins, and iron. Best of all, they are very low in fat. In order to form a complete protein, beans should be combined with whole grains, nuts, seeds, or dairy products.

Dried beans will keep several months when stored in a cool, dry place in a tightly covered container. Once cooked, the beans can be stored for 1 to 2 days in the refrigerator. For longer storage, keep cooked beans in the freezer.

As a general rule, 1 cup of dry beans yields about 2½ cups after cooking. To cook: rinse the beans, remove stones, dirt, and any discolored beans. Cover beans with 3 to 4 times their volume in warm water, and let them soak in the refrigerator overnight or longer. Or, place the beans and water in a large saucepan, bring to a boil, and simmer 5 to 10 minutes. Remove the pan from the heat, cover tightly, and let soak for 2 to 3 hours. The longer the soaking period, the shorter the cooking time. Remember that as beans absorb liquid, they expand!

After soaking, drain the beans, place them in a heavy-bottomed saucepan, cover them with fresh water (1 quart for each 2 cups beans), and bring the beans and water to a boil. Lower the heat and simmer, covered, 1½ to 3 hours, depending on the type of bean. For the beans used in recipes in this book, the best cooking times are as follows:

chick-peas (garbanzo beans)	2½ to 3 hours
kidney beans	1½ to 2 hours
pinto beans	2½ to 3 hours

Because lentils are small and soft-shelled, they need no soaking before cooking. Simply use 3 parts water to 1 part dry lentils and cook until tender, 30 to 60 minutes.

(NOTE: Several soup recipes, such as Tomato Lentil Soup, call for dry lentils which are cooked in the soup stock.)

DRIED BLACK MUSHROOMS

Dried black mushrooms are commonly used in Chinese cooking. They are found in the oriental food sections of supermarkets or at oriental specialty shops, generally packaged in boxes or plastic bags. Stored in tightly closed jars in a cool place, they will keep for up to a year.

Before using dried black mushrooms in recipes such as Garden

Vegetable Stir Fry, reconstitute them by soaking the mushrooms in warm water until they are softened, about 30 minutes. After soaking, use a soft brush to remove sandy particles.

EGG ROLL SKINS

Egg roll skins are, of course, the wrappers used to prepare egg rolls. The dough—made of flour, water, and eggs—is rolled out thinly and cut into squares. To prevent sticking, each square is dusted with cornstarch. I find the Chinese variety of egg roll works best for my recipes. Many supermarkets and most oriental specialty shops stock them in the frozen or refrigerated foods sections.

FLOURS

The recipes in this book call for several types of flour.

Whole wheat flour is made by finely grinding the entire wheat berry. It therefore includes both the germ and the bran. Most whole wheat flour is ground from hard winter wheat, so it has a high content of gluten, a form of protein. Because the gluten allows bread dough to rise and hold its shape, whole wheat flour is a good choice for making whole grain yeast breads.

Whole wheat pastry flour is made from soft spring wheat, which contains less gluten than hard wheat. It is best suited to making pastries, piecrusts, cookies, and quick breads.

Both plain whole wheat and pastry flour are sources of protein, B vitamins, vitamin E, essential fatty acids, and numerous trace minerals. Because the fats can become rancid, these flours should be stored in tightly covered containers in the refrigerator.

Rye flour contains most of the rye berry, and its nutrients are comparable to those found in whole wheat flour. Store in the refrigerator in a covered container. In this book's recipes, rye flour is used in hearty breads and biscuits.

Brown rice flour is made by grinding brown rice. It has a slightly sweet flavor, which makes it especially appropriate for use in pastries. It is high in B vitamins but somewhat lower in protein than is wheat flour.

Soy flour is made from whole soybeans that have been dehulled, cracked, heat treated, and ground into a flour. It is about 20 percent fat and 35 percent protein. To increase the protein in baked goods, use soy flour as a substitute for some of the grain flour. Soy flour is rarely used alone in baked goods because it has a distinct flavor and makes heavy, dense breads, cakes, or pastries.

Before measuring, aerate all flours by stirring. Then, lightly scoop the flour into the measuring cup, taking care not to pack or shake down.

HARUSAME NOODLES (CELLOPHANE NOODLES, BEAN THREAD, *SAIFUN* NOODLES)

Harusame noodles, which are made from mung bean flour and water, are found in the *Harusame* Salad recipe. Prepare the noodles by immersing them in boiling water just long enough to soften them, about 3 minutes. Rinse and chill. Though they have little flavor of their own, *Harusame* noodles make an interesting complement to vegetables and sauces.

HERBAL TEAS

Herbal teas are blends of herbs that can be steeped in water to create pleasantly flavored, healthful beverages. Many companies now package herbal teas in both bulk (loose) and tea-bag form. Most are caffeine free and contain no artificial colorings, flavorings, or preservatives.

My pantry is always stocked with at least 20 different herbal teas. I serve them with the menus in this book. Refreshing, they are an excellent alternative to soft drinks. The entire family will enjoy them.

To prepare herbal teas, I pour boiling water over tea bags or over loose tea in a tea infuser and allow it to steep for 3 to 5 minutes. The longer a tea steeps, the stronger the beverage will be. Honey and a squeeze of lemon or lime are nice additions.

In the summer, I make iced herbal teas. To make my sun tea, I place 4 tea bags in a quart of cold water and allow it to steep in the sunshine for several hours. Iced herbal teas are delicious blended with fruit juices, especially apple juice and orange juice.

JICAMA

Jicama, often called the Mexican potato (and occasionally the Chinese yam), comes from Mexico and other Central American countries, where its status is equal to that of the white potato in the United States. Jicama is a brown tuber resembling a turnip in appearance and a water chestnut in flavor and consistency. In fact, its watery-crisp texture and bland taste are so similar to those of the water chestnut that it makes an excellent substitute for this more expensive vegetable.

When purchasing jicama, look for firm, smooth, clean, well-shaped tubers that are free of cuts and bruises. Small tubers are best because large ones tend to be woody. The interior of a good jicama is white, crisp and juicy.

To use jicama, wash it well and pare it thinly. Slice and use it as a raw vegetable, or cook and serve it in place of a potato. Store fresh jicama in a plastic bag in the refrigerator. It will keep well for one to two weeks.

KEFIR AND KEFIR CHEESE

Kefir is a fermented drink made from milk and a special culture called kefir grains. Kefir cheese, made from kefir, is similar to cream cheese and can be substituted in recipes calling for cream cheese.

Both kefir and kefir cheese can be purchased in natural foods stores and in the dairy sections of some supermarkets. At home, store them in the refrigerator.

LIQUID LECITHIN

Liquid lecithin is an oil extracted from soybeans. It can be purchased in bottled form in natural foods stores and supermarkets. I combine it with safflower oil and use the mixture to oil baking pans. It adds no flavor to baked goods and makes removal of the food from pans easy.

MOLASSES

Molasses is a by-product of the sugar-refining process. Unlike sugar, it contains, in very small amounts, the B vitamins, minerals, and other trace elements such as zinc and copper.

Molasses can be purchased in most supermarkets and natural foods stores. Keep molasses at room temperature before opening; then store in the refrigerator where it will keep for up to 3 months.

NONFAT DRY MILK

Nonfat dry milk is often used to add calcium and protein to baked goods, puddings, and sauces.

Add ⅓ cup powder for each cup of milk or other liquid used in soups, sauces, and beverages, and add ½ cup powder to the dry ingredients in muffins, biscuits, and breads.

NUTS AND SEEDS

Recipes in this book call for nuts and seeds in variety of forms: chopped and added to casseroles, tossed into salads, or ground into a meal or paste and added to baked goods. Seeds are also sprouted and used as a vegetable.

Nuts and seeds are a good source of protein. Because their protein is incomplete, they should be served with grains, dairy products, or legumes for best nutritional value. Most nuts and seeds are high in fat and contain B complex vitamins. Some are good sources of calcium, phosphorous, magnesium, and potassium.

Keep nuts and seeds in tightly covered containers in a cool, dark, and dry area. If I plan to use them readily, I don't store mine in the refrigerator. Refrigerated or frozen, nuts will keep for several months. Several recipes in this book call for raw (unroasted) nuts. Always read labels to see how packaged nuts have been treated; you'll note that sugar, salt, and preservatives are often added.

Most nuts used in the recipes in this book are commonly known, but pine nuts may be new to you. These nuts are found inside the cones of certain pine trees. Their small size and mild flavor make them appropriate for toasting, sautéing, and serving with many vegetables. They are often used in Italian cooking.

I frequently use sesame seeds for their texture and their delicious nutty flavor. Use raw seeds for the recipes in this book unless toasted seeds are specified. To toast sesame seeds, place them in a dry skillet over medium heat and stir for 2 to 5 minutes, or toast them on a dry baking sheet in a 350 °F oven for 8 to 10 minutes, stirring occasionally.

OILS AND OTHER FATS

Oils and fats are a necessary part of our diets. They conserve body heat, help build new tissue, form certain hormones, promote growth of beneficial intestinal bacteria, and carry fat-soluble vitamins (A, D, E, and K) throughout the body.

Many medical experts consider saturated fats dangerous to health because they may contribute to elevated cholesterol levels. At room temperature, saturated fats (such as butter and lard) are usually solid, while unsaturated fats (oils) tend to be liquid.

The nutritional value of oils varies considerably depending on the level of saturation, the degree of freshness, and the extent of processing or refining. Cold-pressed oils, which are labeled as such, are extracted at a lower heat than hot-pressed oils and, therefore, maintain a slightly higher nutritional level. Cold-pressed oils generally contain no preservatives, so they can become rancid. They are best stored in your refrigerator, where they will keep for about 4 months.

Safflower oil is my all-purpose oil for cooking and baking. This cold-pressed oil is fairly light in weight and color and mild in flavor. It has a high enough smoking point to make it suitable for deep-fat frying and sautéing. Safflower oil is the least saturated of all commercial vegetable oils.

Olive oil comes from the fruit of the olive plant. It is frequently used for salads, especially in oil-and-vinegar dressings. It also gives a distinctive flavor to pasta sauces. Because it has a strong flavor, I use olive oil sparingly. Refrigerated olive oil may become cloudy and thick, but it will return to its original state at room temperature without affecting the quality.

Sesame oil is a mild-flavored oil often used in conjunction with other bland oils in order to impart its pleasant flavor. It is available in cold-presssd form, which should be stored under refrigeration.

Corn oil is extracted from the corn germ, the inside part of a kernel of corn. It is my second choice, after safflower oil, as an all-purpose oil. Note that corn oil is more dense and has a tendency to foam in deep-fat frying.

RICE STICKS (*PY MAI FUN*)

Rice sticks are an interesting oriental noodle made of rice and water. They're available in oriental specialty shops and in the oriental foods sections of many supermarkets.

To prepare rice sticks, pour about 2 inches of oil into a deep pan and heat to 375° or 400°F. Break the rice sticks into small pieces about 3 inches long and dip them into the hot oil. The sticks will puff up almost instantly. Remove the cooked noodles with a slotted spoon and place them on a paper towel to drain. Their crisp texture will add interest to salads. Rice sticks can also be boiled for about 3 minutes and used as an accompaniment to an oriental-type stir-fry dish.

SOY SAUCE

Soy sauce is an aged liquid seasoning made from soybeans, water, flour, and salt. It has a high sodium content and therefore should be consumed in limited quantities. Low-sodium soy sauce is now available in many supermarkets. It will keep at room temperature almost indefinitely.

SPROUTS

Sprouted seeds and beans are delicious and nutritious. My favorites for sprouting are alfalfa seeds and mung beans. Sprouts contain varying amounts of protein, calcium, iron, B complex vitamins, and vitamin C, yet they are low in fat and calories. Sprouting is the only process that increases the nutritional value of a food.

When buying seeds for sprouting, make sure that they have not been treated with chemicals. Packages of seeds intended for sprouting are generally labeled as such.

In order to grow sprouts in your kitchen, you will need
- a wide-mouth glass quart jar
- a small piece of cheesecloth or a fine mesh screen
- a rubber band or screw-on jar ring
- 2 tablespoons of seeds per quart
- a warm (70°F), dark storage space

In the jar, soak seeds in a cup of warm water for 8 to 12 hours. Cover the jar opening with the screening material and hold the screen in place with a rubber band or jar ring. Drain off the water, rinse the seeds in lukewarm water, and drain again. Repeat until the water runs clear. Drain throughly and shake the jar to distribute the seeds as evenly as possible. Place the jar on its side in a warm, dark place. Rinse the seeds twice a day. In 3 to 4 days, when the sprouts are 1 to 2 inches long, place the jar in sunlight for a few hours. The light will make the leaves green and increase their vitamin C content.

Store sprouts in the refrigerator, where they will stay fresh for about 4 days. Recipes using sprouts include salads, sandwiches, and garnishes.

TAHINI (SESAME BUTTER)

Tahini, or sesame butter, is a paste made from ground, unhulled sesame seeds. It is a common ingredient in many traditional Middle Eastern dishes.

You can purchase canned tahini in natural foods stores and in some supermarkets. Refrigerate it after opening. Because tahini is neither hydrogenated nor emulsified, its natural oils tend to rise to the surface. Stir the oils back into the butter before using. Tahini is tasty spread on crackers or breads or used as an ingredient in salad dressings, sauces, casseroles, or baked goods.

TOFU

Tofu is a pressed curd consisting of soybeans, water, and a solidifier. It is made by cooking soybeans in water, straining them to extract soy milk, cooking the soy milk, and adding the solidifier to produce curds and whey. The curds are pressed until firm to form cubes.

Tofu cubes are packaged in water and are generally stocked in the produce section of supermarkets and natural foods stores. In some stores, two varieties of tofu are available: firm tofu, which is best used in casseroles, soups, salads, and other recipes calling for distinct cubes; and soft tofu, which contains more liquid and is best used in pureed desserts, dressings, sauces, and dips. Some stores carry unlabeled tofu. This is usually the firm variety. It can be used in recipes requiring a creamy texture, but will require a great deal of mashing.

Tofu is delicious when eaten in combination with other foods. To use tofu, remove it from its storage water and drain. Because it is very absorbent, tofu nicely soaks up the flavor of the surrounding foods and seasonings.

To store, keep tofu refrigerated and submerged in fresh water. If the water is changed daily, tofu will keep for a week. For longer storage, drain and freeze. Unfortunately, tofu that has been frozen and thawed lacks a tender texture. It is best used in casseroles and other dishes in which a chewy texture is desirable.

Tofu is an excellent source of nonmeat protein. To enhance the protein, supplement it with grains, milk, eggs, cheese, nuts, or seeds. Tofu is a good source of iron, low in calories, and cholesterol-free. It also provides B vitamins and calcium. Many people find that it is exceptionally easy to digest.

UNSALTED BUTTER (SWEET BUTTER)

The recipes in this book were developed using unsalted butter. Generally speaking, I prefer unsalted butter because its flavor is more delicate than that of salted butter. Throughout this book, the recipes that call for butter can be prepared using whatever kind of butter you prefer. With recipes that specify unsalted butter, however, you will find that they work much better if it is used.

WHEAT GERM

Wheat germ, which is the heart of the wheat, is rich in protein, B vitamins, vitamin E, potassium, and zinc. For the recipes in this book, I have used it generously to enhance the nutritional value of granola, breads, muffins, cookies, and casseroles. It also imparts a wonderfully nutty flavor to those dishes.

Wheat germ is available in natural foods stores and in supermarkets. It comes in two forms: raw and toasted. Toasted wheat germ has a nuttier taste, is less bitter, and has a longer shelf life than raw wheat germ. Unfortunately, the toasting process lowers nutrient levels. The oil in raw wheat germ tends to become rancid easily so it must be used quickly. Always store raw or toasted wheat germ in an airtight container in the refrigerator or freezer.

Unless toasted is specified, raw wheat germ should be used for recipes in this book. In most other recipes you can substitute wheat germ for part of the flour. For every cup of flour called for in a recipe, use ¾ cup flour and ¼ cup wheat germ.

WILD RICE

Wild rice — actually a grass, not a rice — is native to North America; two-thirds of it is harvested in northern Minnesota. Wild rice contains twice as much protein as white rice, is low in fat, and is a good source of the B complex vitamins. It will keep 6 to 12 months when stored in a tightly covered container in a cool, dry place.

Cook wild rice as you would brown rice. It triples in volume when cooked, so start with less uncooked wild rice per serving than you would regular rice. It has a unique flavor; I often serve it alone or in combination with brown rice.

YOGURT

Yogurt is a cultured milk product with a custardlike consistency and tart flavor. It's a source of protein, fat, carbohydrate, calcium, phosphorus, vitamin A, the B complex vitamins, and vitamin D. Some people believe the bacteria in the yogurt culture acts as an aid to digestion.

To make yogurt, add ⅓ cup nonfat dry milk to 1 quart fresh milk. (Whole, skim, or 2% milk may be used, though the flavor, consistency, and richness will vary with the amount of fat in the milk.) In a stainless steel, glass, or enameled pot, heat the milk to 180°F. Remove the milk from the heat, let it cool to 110°F, and add 1 heaping tablespoon of fresh yogurt with an active culture. Mix well to distribute the starter evenly, but do not beat or whip. Set the mixture aside to incubate at 110° to 115°F.

The easiest way to maintain a constant temperature is in an electric yogurt maker; however, you can also use your oven. Preheat the oven to 250°F, and fill a cake pan with warm water, 110°F. Pour the milk mixture into 4 or 5 small glass or plastic containers. Place these in the pan, put the pan into the oven, and immediately turn off the heat. Leave the containers in the oven or the yogurt maker for 5 to 8 hours. The longer the milk sets, the more tart the flavor of the yogurt. Refrigerate the yogurt for 12 to 24 hours to chill and to continue setting. Frequently, a watery separation will develop. The watery yellowish liquid is whey. It can be poured off before serving for a thicker yogurt, or stirred in for a thinner one.

Though yogurt will keep in the refrigerator for about 10 days, it tastes best when it is fresh. I usually try to use it within a week. Remember to save 1 tablespoon of the yogurt to serve as a starter for your next batch.

There are several reasons why yogurt sometimes fails to become custardlike. The milk may not have been at 110°F when the culture was added; the culture may not have been mixed in throughly; either the milk or the starter culture may have been old; the mixture may have been disturbed during incubation; or the incubation temperature may have been too high or too low.

The recipes in this book call for unflavored (plain) yogurt. Stir in fruits and seasonings to vary the taste of your yogurt.

Back to Basics

Many recipes throughout this book call for such ingredients as mayonnaise, mustard, catsup, vegetable stock, or flavored butters. I've put my favorite recipes for these basics in this chapter so that you too can use them to add special flavor accents to your cooking. The basic granola recipe included here is especially delightful and versatile; I use it as a snack, a breakfast dish, a pie crust ingredient, and a dessert topping. The seasoned croutons enhance salads and casseroles, and the cheese spreads complement whole grain breads, adding to their flavor and their protein level.

Because I don't have the opportunity every day to spend a lot of time cooking, I prepare these basics wherever I have a few extra minutes to do so. All these foods keep nicely for a week or more, and I'm always glad to have a supply of them on hand. It's my way of depositing time when I have it and drawing on it later.

THE BASICS

Butters
- Apple Butter
- Fruit Butters
  - Banana-Pecan Butter
  - Lemon-Honey Butter
  - Orange-Honey Butter
  - Orange-Pineapple Butter
  - Strawberry-Honey Butter
- Herb Butter
- Safflower Butter
- Sweetened Butters
  - Cinnamon-Honey Butter
  - Honey Butter
  - Maple Butter

Condiments
- Catsup
- Mayonnaise
- Mustard
- Orange Honey

Spreads
- Apricot-Apple Spread
- Quick Herb-Cheese Spread
- Ricotta-Orange Spread
- Tangerine Cream Cheese

Other Basics
- Granola
- Lecithin Mixture
- Seasoned Whole Wheat Croutons
- Tomato Hot Sauce
- Vegetable Stock

BUTTERS

APPLE BUTTER

Yields about 2 quarts

- 5 pounds apples, cut into ½-inch chunks
- 1 cup cider vinegar
- 1½ cups honey
- 2 teaspoons ground cinnamon
- 1 teaspoon ground cloves
- rind of 1 lemon, grated
- juice of 1 lemon

Place the apple cubes in a Dutch oven or stock pot. Stir in the vinegar, honey, cinnamon, cloves, lemon rind, and lemon juice.

Cook, covered, over medium heat until the apples are very tender, 20 to 30 minutes. Puree in a food processor or blender.

Return the mixture to the pot and cook over low heat, uncovered, for 1 hour. Stir frequently.

The Apple Butter is done when it is thick and smooth. Cool; then pour into jars and store in the refrigerator.

FRUIT BUTTERS

Yields about 1¾ cups

Flavor	Unsalted Butter, at Room Temperature	Safflower Oil	Honey	Fruit	Spices and Other Flavorings
Banana-Pecan Butter	½ cup	⅓ cup	¼ cup	1 medium-size banana, mashed	1 teaspoon lemon juice 1 teaspoon ground cinnamon (optional) 3 tablespoons finely chopped pecans
Lemon-Honey Butter	½ cup	⅓ cup	¼ cup	2 teaspoons lemon juice	1 teaspoon grated lemon rind
Orange-Honey Butter	½ cup	⅓ cup	¼ cup	2 teaspoons orange juice	rind of 1 orange, grated
Orange-Pineapple Butter	½ cup	⅓ cup	¼ cup	½ cup crushed pineapple, drained	1 tablespoon grated orange rind
Strawberry-Honey Butter	½ cup	⅓ cup	¼ cup	1 cup fresh strawberries, sliced	rind of 1 orange, grated

Beat butter until light and fluffy. Beating continuously, gradually add oil and blend thoroughly. Beat in honey, fruit, spices, and other flavorings.

Store in a covered container in the refrigerator. These butters will keep for 1 week.

HERB BUTTER

½ cup unsalted butter, at room
    temperature
⅓ cup safflower oil
1 clove garlic, crushed
½ teaspoon finely chopped fresh
    parsley
½ teaspoon finely chopped fresh
    chives
½ teaspoon dried dill weed
    dash of pepper
    dash of lemon juice
1 tablespoon grated Parmesan
    cheese (optional)

In a small bowl beat butter until light and fluffy. Beating continuously, add oil until thoroughly blended, then add remaining ingredients.

Store in a covered jar or crock in the refrigerator.

SAFFLOWER BUTTER

Yields about 1 cup

½ cup unsalted butter, at room
    temperature
⅓ cup safflower oil

Whip the butter until smooth and fluffy. Continue beating and gradually add the oil.

Pour into a container, cover, and store in the refrigerator.

Even when chilled, this butter will remain spreadable. Use it as an all-purpose spread and for sautéing.

SWEETENED BUTTERS

Yields 1 to 1½ cups

Flavor	Unsalted Butter, at Room Temperature	Safflower Oil	Sweetener	Spices
Honey Butter	½ cup	⅓ cup	¼ cup honey	—
Cinnamon-Honey Butter	½ cup	⅓ cup	¼ cup honey	½ teaspoon ground cinnamon ⅛ teaspoon ground nutmeg
Maple Butter	½ cup	⅓ cup	¼ cup maple syrup	—

Beat butter until light and fluffy. Gradually beat in oil, blending thoroughly. Continue beating and add sweetener and spices, if any.

Store in a covered container in the refrigerator. These butters will keep for 1 week.

CONDIMENTS

CATSUP

Yields about 2 cups

1½ cups (15-ounce can) tomato
    puree
½ cup cider vinegar
¼ cup honey
1 tablespoon chopped onion
½ teaspoon dry mustard
½ teaspoon ground cinnamon
½ teaspoon ground allspice
½ teaspoon celery seed
¼ teaspoon pepper
⅛ teaspoon garlic powder
    pinch of cayenne pepper

Combine all ingredients in a medium-size saucepan; bring to a boil. Reduce heat to low and simmer for 15 minutes.

Store in a covered container in the refrigerator. Stir before using.

MAYONNAISE

Yields 2 cups

2 eggs
4 tablespoons cider vinegar
1 tablespoon honey
¼ teaspoon white pepper
1½ cups safflower oil

In blender or food processor, process all ingredients except oil until smooth. Continue processing and add the oil very slowly, until well mixed and thick.

The Mayonnaise will keep 2 weeks in the refrigerator.

MUSTARD

Yields 2½ cups

1 cup (4-ounce can) dry mustard
1 cup cider vinegar
3 large eggs
¾ cup honey

Sterilize glass containers to accommodate 2½ cups of Mustard.

In a small bowl, combine mustard and vinegar; whisk to remove lumps. Cover and let stand overnight.

Pour the mustard-vinegar mixture into a blender or food processor. Add the eggs and honey; process until smooth.

Transfer the mixture to the top of a double boiler; cook, stirring constantly, until mixture reaches pudding consistency, about 15 minutes.

Pour into containers and refrigerate.

For sweeter Mustard, use 1 cup honey.

ORANGE HONEY

Yields about ½ cup

½ cup honey
2 tablespoons orange juice
3 teaspoons grated orange rind

Combine all ingredients, cover, and refrigerate. Drizzle over warm muffins.

SPREADS

APRICOT-APPLE SPREAD

Yields about 1½ cups

1 6-ounce can apple juice
   concentrate
1½ cups apple juice
1½ cups chopped dried apricots
1 tablespoon lemon juice
¼ teaspoon almond extract
¼ teaspoon ground cinnamon

In a saucepan, combine the apple juice concentrate, apple juice, and apricots. Bring mixture to a boil; reduce the heat and simmer uncovered, stirring occasionally, until the apricots are very tender and most of the liquid has been absorbed, about 40 minutes.

Remove from heat; cool partially. Puree in a food processor or blender. Stir in the lemon juice, almond extract, and cinnamon.

Store in a covered jar in the refrigerator.

QUICK HERB-CHEESE SPREAD

Yields about 1 cup

½ pound kefir cheese or cream
   cheese, at room temperature
1 clove garlic, minced
1 tablespoon minced fresh parsley
1 teaspoon caraway seed
1 teaspoon dried basil
1 teaspoon fresh chives
   dash of soy sauce
   dash of freshly ground pepper

Combine ingredients in a small bowl and blend thoroughly. Cover and chill for 8 to 12 hours to allow flavors to blend.

Serve with biscuits, muffins, or crackers.

RICOTTA-ORANGE SPREAD

Yields 1 cup

1 cup ricotta cheese
1 tablespoon honey
2 teaspoons grated orange rind

Combine all ingredients and chill.

TANGERINE CREAM CHEESE

Yields about 1 cup

½ cup cream cheese or kefir cheese,
   at room temperature
2 tablespoons unsalted butter, at
   room temperature
2 tablespoons tangerine or orange
   juice
1 tablespoon honey
1 teaspoon lemon juice
1 tablespoon grated tangerine or
   orange rind

Beat the cheese and butter until light and fluffy. Add the juice, honey, and lemon juice; continue beating. Stir in the rind.

Cover and refrigerate.

OTHER BASICS

GRANOLA

Yields 16 cups

4 cups rolled oats
1 cup slivered almonds or coarsely
   chopped pecans
1 cup bran
1 cup sunflower seeds
1 cup soy flour
1 cup shredded unsweetened
   coconut
1 cup nonfat dry milk
1 cup wheat germ
⅔ cup sesame seeds
2 tablespoons lecithin powder
1 cup honey, warmed
1 cup safflower oil
1 teaspoon vanilla extract
1 cup raisins (or prunes, dates,
   dried apples, or apricots)

Preheat oven to 300°F.

In a large bowl, place the oats, almonds or pecans, bran, sunflower seeds, soy flour, coconut, dry milk, wheat germ, sesame seeds, and lecithin. Stir to combine well.

In a small bowl, combine honey, oil, and vanilla. Add to the dry mixture, tossing until well blended.

Spread mixture evenly on 2 baking sheets.

Bake, stirring frequently, until lightly browned, about 45 minutes. Loosen the Granola from the baking sheets with a spatula. Sprinkle with raisins or other dried fruit and allow to cool. (The Granola will become crisper as it cools.)

Store the Granola in covered containers. Serve with milk or yogurt and fresh fruit.

LECITHIN MIXTURE

Yields 1 cup

⅔ cup safflower oil
⅓ cup liquid lecithin

Stir together the oil and lecithin; store in a covered jar in the refrigerator.

Use this mixture for oiling baking pans. It adds no flavor to baked goods and makes their removal from pans easy. It also simplifies clean up.

SEASONED WHOLE WHEAT CROUTONS

Yields 2 cups

3 tablespoons butter
1½ tablespoons safflower oil
2 cloves garlic, minced
½ teaspoon dried basil
½ teaspoon dried oregano
2 cups whole wheat bread cubes

Heat butter and oil in heavy skillet. Add the garlic, basil, and oregano; sauté 1 minute, stirring constantly. Stir in the bread cubes and sauté until browned and crisp.

TOMATO HOT SAUCE

Yields 1¾ cups

2 medium-size tomatoes, peeled and chopped
¼ cup chopped onion
¼ cup chopped celery
¼ cup chopped green pepper
½ cup (4-ounce can) minced green chilies (seeds removed for milder flavor)
¼ cup tomato paste
2 tablespoons safflower oil
½ teaspoon ground coriander
¼ teaspoon pepper
4 drops hot pepper sauce

In a food processor or blender, puree the tomatoes, onion, celery, and green pepper.

Transfer the pureed mixture to a medium-size saucepan and add the remaining ingredients. Bring to a boil, reduce the heat, and simmer, uncovered, for 20 minutes, stirring occasionally. Store in a covered jar in the refrigerator. Serve at room temperature.

This sauce is tastiest when made a few days in advance so that the flavors have a chance to blend.

VEGETABLE STOCK

- 4 tablespoon safflower oil or butter
- 2 large onions, chopped
- 3 large carrots, chopped
- 12 green beans, cut into 1-inch pieces
- 4 stalks celery, chopped
- 3 medium-size tomatoes, cubed
- 1 potato, cubed
- ½ pound spinach, chopped
- 2 leeks, sliced
- 1 turnip, chopped
- 2 cloves garlic, minced
- 3 quarts water or liquid from cooking vegetables
- 10 peppercorns
- 1 bay leaf
- 6 sprigs of parsley
- 1 teaspoon dried thyme leaves
- 1 teaspoon dried basil
- 3 tablespoons soy sauce
- 1 teaspoon freshly ground pepper

In a stock pot, heat the oil or melt the butter. Add the onions, carrots, green beans, celery, tomatoes, potato, spinach, leeks, turnip, and garlic. Cook until the vegetables are tender, about 10 minutes.

Add water or cooking liquid and remaining ingredients. Cover, bring to a boil, reduce the heat and simmer 1½ to 2 hours.

Strain the stock and discard the vegetables. Use the stock immediately, keep in the refrigerator for 2 to 3 days, or freeze for up to a month.

MENUS AND RECIPES

Breakfasts and Brunches

Breakfast fuels your day's activity, so I say, make it substantial. The wide variety of foods that can get the day off and running gives me plenty of inspiration for interesting meals — granola, pancakes, frittatas, stewed fruit, blintzes. Brunch, a combined breakfast and lunch, is a delightfully convenient way to entertain; some of my favorite and most successful parties have featured brunches. Dishes akin to those served for breakfasts and lunches — Vegetable Frittata, Carrot-Corn Muffins, Broccoli-Almond Soufflé Roll — work superbly for brunches.

Included in this chapter are both do-ahead menus and those best cooked on the spot. Many are also appropriate for luncheons and light suppers. Each menu includes a combination of fruit, grain, and vegetable dishes. The fruit dishes are scrumptious as a first course or as a breakfast dessert.

I know you will enjoy beginning the day for yourself, your family, and your friends with these creative, inviting menus.

MENUS
BREAKFASTS AND BRUNCHES

ɣ Morning Punch
   Granola Banana Splits
   Orange Bran Muffins

ɣ Hot Spiced Cider
   Tofu-Nut Pancake Sundaes with Vanilla Yogurt and Maple-Baked Pears

ɣ Orange Juliet
   Whole Grain Hot Cereal with Apricot-Orange or Papaya-Orange Sauce
   Peanut Butter-Oatmeal Muffins

ɣ Cranberry Special
   Broiled Grapefruit
   Asparagus Toast
   Granola Bars

ɣ Strawberry Frappé
   Eggs Florentine
   Banana-Apricot Bread

ɣ Hot Apple Tea
   Vegetable Frittata
   Carrot Corn Muffins
   Stewed Fruit and Yogurt

𝒴 Hot Spiced Tomato Juice
Vegetable-Cheese Strata with Baked Sauced Mushrooms
Crusty Rye Bread
Fresh Fruit Ambrosia

𝒴 Fruit Blend Supreme
Whole Wheat-Cheese Blintzes with Cranberry Applesauce

𝒴 Sunrise Vegetable Soup
Savory Spinach-Stuffed Eggs with Mushroom-Shallot Sauce
Pineapple-Pecan Muffins
Honey-Baked Gingered Pears and Almond Stuffing

𝒴 Warming Grape-Cinnnamon Punch
Broiled Pineapple
Poached Eggs and Spinach with Yogurt Hollandaise

𝒴 Hot Spiced Pineapple Juice
Broccoli-Almond Soufflé Roll with Spanish Basque Sauce
Irish Soda Bread

BEVERAGES

CRANBERRY SPECIAL

Yields 1 quart

- 4 cups cranberries
- 4½ cups water
- ½ cup honey
- 2 tablespoons lemon juice

Place cranberries and water in a large saucepan. Cook over medium heat until skins pop and berries are soft, about 15 minutes. Strain; add honey to the hot liquid and stir until dissolved. Add the lemon juice.

Serve warm or chill 1 hour and serve over ice.

The cooked berries make tasty additions to breads, muffins, or fruit salads and are especially delightful when pureed, sweetened with honey, and served in place of applesauce.

FRUIT BLEND SUPREME

Yields about 1½ quarts

- 2 medium-size bananas, mashed
- 2 eggs
- 2 cups milk
- 1½ cups apricot juice
- 1½ cups pineapple juice
- 4 tablespoons nonfat dry milk

Place all ingredients in a food processor or blender; process until smooth. Serve plain or with crushed ice.

HOT APPLE TEA

Yields 1 quart

- 1 quart apple juice
- 4 teaspoons loose (or 4 bags) mild-flavored herbal tea
- apple slices
- lemon slices

In a 1½-quart saucepan, bring the apple juice to a boil. Pour into a large teapot; brew tea in the hot juice for about 5 minutes.

Serve hot, and garnish with an apple slice and a lemon slice in each cup.

HOT SPICED CIDER

1 teaspoon whole cloves
1 teaspoon whole allspice
1 stick of cinnamon
1 quart apple juice
¼ cup honey
  orange slices

Wrap cloves, allspice, and cinnamon in a cheesecloth bag or place in a large tea infuser.

In a medium-size saucepan, combine juice and honey. Add the bag of spices and bring to a boil. Add the orange slices. Reduce heat to medium, cover, and simmer for 20 minutes.

Remove spices. Serve warm; ladle cider into mugs and top each with an orange slice.

HOT SPICED PINEAPPLE JUICE

Yields about 1½ quarts

6 cups pineapple juice
¼ cup lemon juice
¼ teaspoon ground allspice
¼ teaspoon ground cinnamon
¼ teaspoon ground nutmeg

Combine all ingredients in a medium-size saucepan; bring to a boil over medium heat. Reduce heat, cover, and simmer for 15 minutes. Serve warm in mugs.

HOT SPICED TOMATO JUICE

Yields about 1½ quarts

6 cups tomato juice
⅓ cup honey
10 whole cloves
2 sticks of cinnamon
3 stalks celery, with leaves, sliced
¼ cup lemon juice
  pepper, to taste

Combine tomato juice, honey, cloves, cinnamon, and celery in a 1½ quart saucepan. Cover and simmer 15 minutes. Strain and return to saucepan. Stir in lemon juice; add pepper. Reheat, but do not bring to a boil.

Ladle into mugs and serve immediately.

MORNING PUNCH

Yields about 2 quarts

4 cups apple juice, chilled
2 cups pineapple juice, chilled
1 cup orange juice, chilled
½ cup lemon juice, chilled
   lemon slices

Combine the juices. Garnish each serving with a thin slice of lemon.

ORANGE JULIET

Yields 3 cups

2 cups orange juice
½ cup nonfat dry milk
4 ice cubes
¼ teaspoon vanilla extract

Place all ingredients in a food processor or blender; process until smooth. Serve immediately.

STRAWBERRY FRAPPÉ

Yields about 3 cups

2 cups orange juice
1 cup fresh strawberries
2 tablespoons lemon juice
   mint sprigs

In a blender, process orange juice, strawberries, and lemon juice until strawberries are pureed and mixture is smooth. Serve over crushed ice in stemmed glasses. Garnish each serving with a sprig of mint.

WARMING GRAPE-CINNAMON PUNCH

Yields about 1¼ quarts

4 cups white grape juice
2 cups water
1 tablespoon honey
2 sticks of cinnamon
   lemon slices

Combine all ingredients in a medium-size saucepan. Warm over medium heat; remove cinnamon sticks and ladle into mugs. Top each serving with a lemon slice.

MAIN COURSES

ASPARAGUS TOAST

4 servings

4   tablespoons butter
2   tablespoons whole wheat flour
1   cup milk
1   cup grated cheddar cheese
    (4 ounces)
½   teaspoon dry mustard
    dash of cayenne pepper
6   eggs, beaten
2   tablespoons cold water
¼   cup cottage cheese
¼   teaspoon pepper
4   slices whole wheat bread, toasted
16 to 20   asparagus spears, steamed and
    kept warm
1   large tomato, at room
    temperature, cut into 4 slices
    rind of 1 orange, grated (optional)
    dash of paprika (optional)

Melt 2 tablespoons of the butter in a medium-size saucepan. Remove from the heat and blend in the flour. Return to medium heat and cook, stirring constantly, until mixture is smooth and bubbly. Remove from heat again; stir in milk. Return to medium heat and cook, stirring constantly, until mixture is thick and smooth. Do not allow the mixture to boil. Add cheese, mustard, and cayenne; continue to stir until the cheese has melted. Cover, set aside, and keep warm.

In a medium-size bowl, combine the eggs, water, cottage cheese, and pepper.

Melt another 2 tablespoons butter in a skillet. Pour in the egg mixture and scramble until cooked but not dry. Cover and keep warm.

To assemble: spoon a layer of scrambled eggs onto each slice of whole wheat toast. Arrange 4 or 5 asparagus spears on the eggs, add a tomato slice, and pour cheese sauce over the top. Garnish each with grated orange rind or paprika.

GRANOLA BANANA SPLITS

1 serving

¼   cup Granola (page 33)
½   cup yogurt (page 24)
½   cup bananas (or pineapple,
    cantaloupe, strawberries,
    peaches, blueberries, or a
    combination), sliced
2   tablespoons raisins
1   tablespoon maple syrup
1   tablespoon toasted wheat germ
2   tablespoons slivered almonds
1   tablespoon unsweetened coconut

For each serving, layer the ingredients in a cereal bowl in the order given.

This recipe is only a guideline; vary the ingredients and quantities to suit your preference.

BROCCOLI-ALMOND SOUFFLÉ ROLL WITH
SPANISH BASQUE SAUCE

6 servings

1 **pound broccoli**
4 **tablespoons butter**
¾ **cup whole wheat pastry flour**
1 **teaspoon dry mustard**
3 **cups milk**
4 **eggs, separated**
¾ **cup sliced almonds**
½ **teaspoon dried thyme leaves**
  dash of nutmeg
½ **cup shredded cheddar cheese**
   (2 ounces)
   Spanish Basque Sauce (see
   following recipe)

Divide the broccoli into small florets and thinly slice the stems. Steam until tender, 4 to 6 minutes. Chop the broccoli and set aside.

Preheat oven to 325°F. Oil the bottom and sides of a 10 × 15-inch jelly-roll pan. Then, line the bottom of the pan with aluminum foil. Butter and lightly flour the foil; set pan aside.

In a medium-size saucepan, melt 2 tablespoons of the butter over medium heat. Stir in the flour and mustard. Cook, stirring, until bubbly. Gradually pour in the milk; cook, stirring often, until the sauce is smooth and thick, 8 to 10 minutes. Measure 1 cup of this sauce and set aside. Allow sauce to cool.

Beat the egg yolks lightly and gradually beat in all but the 1 cup of reserved sauce. Beat the egg whites until stiff; fold gently into the yolk mixture. Pour into the jelly-roll pan.

Bake until the soufflé is lightly browned and the center springs back when touched, 35 to 40 minutes.

While the soufflé, is baking, melt the remaining butter in a large skillet. Add the almonds and sauté stirring frequently, until lightly toasted. Add broccoli, thyme, and nutmeg; mix.

Heat the reserved cup of sauce; add the cheese and stir until melted. Combine this sauce with the broccoli-almond mixture.

When the soufflé is done, loosen it gently around the edges with a spatula and invert it onto a clean towel. Starting at one narrow edge spread the broccoli mixture over three-fourths of the soufflé. Using the towel for support, roll the soufflé to enclose the filling. Place onto a serving platter, seam side down.

To serve, cut into 6 slices. Pour Spanish Basque Sauce over each.

If not served immediately, the Soufflé Roll may be held in a 200°F oven for up to 30 minutes.

Spanish Basque Sauce

2 medium-size onions, minced
1 green pepper, minced
1 cup sliced mushrooms
1 cup cooked tomatoes, mashed
2 stalks celery, minced
1 bay leaf
1 clove garlic, minced
1 teaspoon dried basil
½ teaspoon dried oregano
½ teaspoon pepper
⅔ cup (6-ounce can) tomato paste
½ cup tomato juice

Combine all ingredients in a Dutch oven or large saucepan. Bring to a boil; reduce heat and simmer, covered, until vegetables are tender, about 30 minutes. (For a thinner sauce, more tomato juice may be added at this time.)

Delicious served over the Broccoli-Almond Soufflé Roll as well as omelets.

EGGS FLORENTINE

4 servings

2 pounds spinach
1 tablespoon lemon juice
¼ teaspoon ground nutmeg
2 tablespoons butter
2 tablespoons whole wheat flour
1 clove garlic, minced
1 cup milk
¼ cup grated Swiss cheese (1 ounce)
¼ teaspoon pepper
8 eggs
½ cup freshly grated Parmesan
    cheese (2 ounces)

Rinse the spinach. In a large saucepan, cook the spinach, covered, without water except for the drops that cling to the leaves. Reduce heat when steam forms and cook 2 to 3 minutes. Drain, squeeze dry, and chop. Place in a bowl and add the lemon juice and nutmeg. Set aside.

Preheat oven to 350°F. Oil a shallow 6 × 10-inch baking dish.

In a small saucepan, melt the butter, sprinkle with the flour and garlic; cook, stirring constantly, for 1 minute. Gradually stir in the milk; bring to a boil, stirring constantly. Cook until thickened, about 1 minute. Add the Swiss cheese and pepper; stir until the cheese has melted. Stir half of this sauce into the spinach.

Spread the spinach mixture in the baking dish. With the back of a spoon, make 8 depressions in the spinach mixture and break 1 egg into each hole. Spoon 1 tablespoon of the remaining sauce over each egg, sprinkle with the Parmesan, and bake until the eggs are set, 10 to 15 minutes. Serve immediately.

POACHED EGGS AND SPINACH WITH YOGURT HOLLANDAISE

4 servings

Yogurt Hollandaise (see following recipe)
1 **pound mushrooms, sliced**
6 **tablespoons butter**
2 **pounds spinach**
4 **whole grain English muffins**
8 **eggs**
   paprika

Prepare the Yogurt Hollandaise; keep warm in the top of a double boiler. Sauté the mushrooms in 4 tablespoons of the butter; remove from heat. Cover to keep warm.

Rinse the spinach. In a large saucepan, cook the spinach, covered, without water except for the drops that cling to the leaves. Reduce heat when steam forms and cook 2 to 3 minutes. Drain, squeeze dry, and chop. Keep warm.

Split and toast the English muffins; butter lightly. Keep warm.

To poach the eggs: Fill a large skillet with 1½ inches of water. Bring water to a gentle boil over medium heat. Break an egg into a saucer. With a spoon, swirl water to make a small circle. Slip the egg into the circle. Repeat with the remaining eggs. When all eggs are in the pan, gently spoon the hot water over the top of each egg to cook the top surface. When the whites are set, but the yolks still soft, remove the eggs from the water with a slotted spoon. Drain briefly on paper towels.

To assemble Poached Eggs and Spinach: Spread a layer of spinach on each half of the toasted and buttered muffins. Arrange a layer of the sautéed mushrooms. Place 1 egg on top of each. Pour Yogurt Hollandaise on each serving; spinkle with paprika. Serve immediately.

NOTE: Keeping the ingredients warm is a challenge when making this recipe. If desired, the eggs may be poached in advance. To reheat, immerse the eggs in a generous amount of water just hot to the touch, but not hot enough to cook the eggs. Allow the eggs to stand 5 to 10 minutes in the hot bath.

Yogurt Hollandaise

1 cup yogurt (page 24)
2 whole eggs, beaten
2 egg yolks, lightly beaten
2 tablespoons butter
1 teaspoon lemon juice
1 teaspoon soy sauce
½ teaspoon Mustard (page 31)
½ teaspoon honey
 dash of white pepper
 dash of cayenne pepper

In top of a double boiler, mix all ingredients. Cook, over barely simmering water, stirring constantly, until thick, 8 to 10 minutes. Serve hot.

If made ahead, reheat, stirring constantly, in top of double boiler over hot, not boiling, water.

VEGETABLE FRITTATA

4 to 6 servings

4 tablespoons safflower oil
1 medium-size green pepper, cut into julienne strips
1 medium-size red pepper, cut into julienne strips
¼ cup chopped scallions
1 clove garlic, minced
4 small new potatoes, thinly sliced
6 eggs, beaten
¾ cup freshley grated Parmesan cheese (3 ounces)
2 tablespoons milk
⅛ teaspoon pepper
 pinch of dried basil
 pinch of dried oregano

In a large skillet, heat the oil over medium heat; add the peppers, scallions, and garlic; sauté, stirring occasionally. After 15 minutes, add potatoes; cover and cook over low heat until potatoes are tender, 5 to 10 minutes.

Meanwhile, in a medium-size bowl, combine the eggs, ¼ cup Parmesan, milk, pepper, basil, and oregano. When the potatoes are cooked, pour the egg mixture over the cooked vegetables.

Turn heat to the lowest setting and cook until eggs are nearly set, but the tops are still runny, 10 to 15 minutes. Turn the frittata, moist side down, onto a buttered plate: then, slide it back into the pan to lightly brown the other side. Or, if the skillet has a heat-resistant handle, brown under the broiler. Slice into wedges and serve immediately with the remaining cheese.

SAVORY SPINACH-STUFFED EGGS WITH
MUSHROOM-SHALLOT SAUCE

6 to 8 servings

12 hard-cooked eggs
½ pound spinach
1 tablespoon butter
¼ pound firm tofu, drained
   and mashed
12 mushroom stems, chopped
2 tablespoons wheat germ
1 clove garlic, minced
1 tablespoon chopped fresh parsley
1 tablespoon soy sauce
   dash of white pepper
   Mushroom-Shallot Sauce (see
   following recipe)

Preheat oven to 350°F. Oil a shallow 9×9-inch baking pan.

Cut the eggs in half lengthwise. Remove the yolks and mash them with a fork. Set aside. Arrange the whites, cut side up, in the prepared pan.

Rinse the spinach. In a medium-size saucepan, cook the spinach, covered, without water except for the drops that cling to the leaves. Reduce heat when steam forms and cook 2 to 3 minutes. Drain, squeeze dry, and chop. Keep warm.

Melt the butter in a 1½-quart saucepan. Add the spinach, tofu, mushrooms, wheat germ, garlic, parsley, soy sauce, and white pepper. Cook over medium heat for 10 minutes, stirring occasionally. Stir in reserved egg yolks. Stuff each halved egg with this mixture.

Pour the Mushroom-Shallot Sauce over the stuffed eggs. Bake until heated through, about 20 minutes.

Mushroom-Shallot Sauce

Yields about 2½ cups

6 tablespoons butter
2 cups minced mushroom caps
2 tablespoons chopped shallots
4 tablespoons whole wheat flour
2 cups milk
   dash of ground nutmeg

In a medium-size saucepan, melt 2 tablespoons of the butter. Sauté mushrooms and shallots until tender but not browned. Remove from saucepan and set aside.

In the saucepan, melt the remaining butter. Remove from heat; stir in the flour; return to heat and cook until mixture is smooth and bubbly. Remove from heat; stir in milk. Return to heat and stir until mixture is smooth and thickened.

Stir in the sautéed mushrooms and shallots, and the nutmeg.

TOFU-NUT PANCAKE SUNDAES WITH
VANILLA YOGURT AND MAPLE-BAKED PEARS

6 servings

3 eggs
½ cup cottage cheese (4 ounces)
1 cup firm tofu, drained
¼ cup milk
3 tablespoons whole wheat flour
2 tablespoons finely chopped
    almonds
2 tablespoons wheat germ
½ teaspoon baking soda
    dash of ground nutmeg
2 tablespoons safflower oil,
    for frying
¼ cup poppy seeds
    Vanilla Yogurt (see accompany-
        ing recipe)
    Maple-Baked Pears (see
        accompanying recipe)

In a blender or food processor, combine eggs, cottage cheese, tofu, milk, flour, almonds, wheat germ, baking soda, and nutmeg. Blend well. Check the consistency of the batter, and add more milk if too thick.

Oil a griddle well and heat. Sprinkle 1 teaspoon of poppy seeds where each pancake is to be cooked, then spoon on the batter. Cook over medium heat until bubbles rise and begin to break; turn and cook other side.

On each plate place 3 pancakes in a circle, edges overlapping. In the center place ½ cup Vanilla Yogurt. Top with a generous helping of Maple-Baked Pears. Drizzle with the pear juice and maple syrup which has accumulated in the baking dish. Serve with additional heated maple syrup, if desired.

Vanilla Yogurt

Yields 3 cups

3 cups yogurt (page 24)
1 tablespoon vanilla extract
3 tablespoons maple syrup

Combine all ingredients; chill.

Maple-Baked Pears

6 servings

6 pears
⅓ cup maple syrup
1 teaspoon vanilla extract
½ cup sliced almonds
¼ cup wheat germ
2 tablespoons butter

Preheat oven to 350°F. Oil a 9 ×9-inch baking dish. Slice pears in ¼-inch-thick wedges. Arrange in rows in the baking dish.

Mix syrup and vanilla; drizzle this mixture over the pears. Sprinkle with almonds and wheat germ; dot with butter.

Bake, basting occasionally with the juices that accumulate, until pears are tender, 10 to 15 minutes.

VEGETABLE-CHEESE STRATA WITH BAKED SAUCED MUSHROOMS

6 servings

2 stalks celery, chopped
1 cup cauliflower florets
1 cup broccoli florets
¼ cup chopped green pepper
3 eggs beaten
1½ cups milk
1 tablespoon soy sauce
¼ teaspoon dry mustard
¼ teaspoon pepper
8 slices whole wheat bread, cubed
1½ cups shredded cheddar cheese
    (6 ounces)
    Baked Sauced Mushrooms (see
    following recipe)

In a large saucepan, combine celery, cauliflower, broccoli, and green pepper; steam until crisp-tender.

In a small bowl, mix eggs, milk, soy sauce, mustard, and pepper.

Oil a 1½-quart baking dish or soufflé dish. In the baking dish, layer ½ the bread cubes, ½ the cheese, and the steamed vegetables. Top with remaining cheese, then the remaining bread. Pour the egg mixture over the layers. Cover and refrigerate 6 hours or overnight.

Preheat oven to 350°F.

Bake the strata, uncovered, for 1 hour. Allow to stand 10 minutes; spoon onto plates and top with Baked Sauced Mushrooms.

Baked Sauced Mushrooms

6 servings

4 tablespoons butter
2 tablespoons whole wheat flour
½ cup sour half-and-half or sour
    cream
¾ cup milk
2 tablespoons minced onion
1 tablespoon lemon juice
2 tablespoons chopped fresh parsley
¼ teaspoon pepper
    dash of ground nutmeg
½ pound small mushrooms
¼ cup whole grain bread crumbs

Preheat oven to 350°F. Oil a 1-quart casserole dish.

In a small saucepan, melt 3 tablespoons of the butter; stir in the flour until smooth. Add the half-and-half or sour cream and milk; stir until creamy. Bring mixture to a boil, stirring constantly; remove from heat.

Stir in onion, lemon juice, parsley, pepper, and nutmeg. Add mushrooms, and stir until all vegetables are coated with the cream mixture. Spoon the mixture into the prepared casserole. Bake for 25 minutes.

While the mushrooms are baking, melt the remaining butter in a small skillet. Stir in the bread crumbs; set aside.

When the mushrooms have been baked for 25 minutes, sprinkle them with the buttered bread crumbs. Bake an additional 5 minutes.

Spoon the Baked Sauced Mushrooms over individual servings of Vegetable-Cheese Strata.

WHOLE GRAIN HOT CEREAL WITH
APRICOT-ORANGE OR PAPAYA-ORANGE SAUCE

4 servings

1½ cups milk
1 tablespoon honey
¼ cup whole wheat cream of wheat
¼ cup rolled oats
¼ cup golden raisins
2 tablespoons wheat germ
1 tablespoon butter
1 egg, beaten
¼ teaspoon vanilla extract
4 tablespoons sliced almonds
One of the following:
    Apricot-Orange Sauce (see accompanying recipe)
    Papaya-Orange Sauce (see accompanying recipe)
1½ cups chopped fresh fruit (pears, bananas, or apples)

Combine milk and honey in a heavy saucepan; bring to a boil; reduce heat. Add the wheat, oats, raisins, and wheat germ. Cook over low heat, stirring constantly, until mixture is thick and smooth, about 10 minutes. Stir in butter. Remove pan from heat and stir in the egg, mixing thoroughly. Stir in vanilla.

Spoon into 4 cereal bowls; sprinkle each with 1 tablespoon sliced almonds.

Serve immediately with warm Apricot-Orange Sauce, warm Papaya-Orange Sauce, or chopped fresh fruit.

Apricot-Orange Sauce

Yields 1¾ cups

½ cup dry apricots, loosely packed
1¾ cups orange juice
¼ teaspoon ground nutmeg

Place the apricots and ½ cup orange juice in a medium-size saucepan. Bring to a boil; reduce heat to low, cover, and simmer until apricots are very soft, about 20 minutes.

Pour apricot-orange mixture into a food processor or blender. Add remaining orange juice and nutmeg. Process until very smooth.

Apricot-Orange Sauce is a terrific topping for hot cereals, pancakes, spiced cakes, yogurt, or ice cream.

Papaya-Orange Sauce

Yields about 1 cup

1 papaya, cubed
½ cup orange juice
2 tablespoons honey
2 tablespoons melted butter
1 teaspoon ground cinnamon
dash of ground nutmeg

Place all ingredients in a food processor or blender; process until very smooth.

Serve warm or chilled on hot cereal, pancakes, spiced cakes, yogurt, or ice cream.

WHOLE WHEAT-CHEESE BLINTZES WITH CRANBERRY APPLESAUCE

Makes 12 blintzes

8 ounces dry-curd cottage cheese
¼ cup kefir cheese or cream cheese (2 ounces)
1 egg yolk
½ tablespoon melted butter
½ tablespoon honey
½ tablespoon lemon juice
1 tablespoon grated lemon rind
¼ teaspoon vanilla extract
   dash of ground nutmeg
2 eggs
1 cup water
⅓ cup whole wheat pastry flour
2 tablespoons butter
   yogurt (page 24)
   Cranberry Applesauce (see following recipe)

In a medium-size bowl, mix cottage cheese, kefir cheese or cream cheese, egg yolk, melted butter, honey, lemon juice, lemon rind, vanilla, and nutmeg. Set aside.

In a food processor or blender, process the eggs, water, and flour until blended. Heat a lightly oiled 6-inch skillet over medium-high heat. Pour a scant ¼ cup of batter into the skillet, and tilt the pan so that the batter spreads evenly over the bottom. Pour off any excess batter, so that only a thin layer is left in the skillet. Cook until the edges begin to pull away from the pan. (The top of the blintze may still look moist.) Turn out, cooked side up, by inverting the skillet over a board.

Whisk the batter occasionally and repeat the steps for cooking a blintze until all batter has been used. If blintzes begin sticking to the pan, oil lightly again.

Drain any excess liquid which may have accumulated in the cheese mixture. Place 1 to 2 tablespoons of cheese mixture at one end of the cooked side of each blintze. Fold in the sides like an envelope, and roll up gently from the filled end to form 2 × 2-inch squares.

Melt butter in a large skillet. Cook blintzes until lightly browned on both sides. Serve hot with yogurt and Cranberry Applesauce.

Cranberry Applesauce

Yields about 2 cups

3 medium-size apples, cubed
1 cup cranberries
2 tablespoons apple juice
2 tablespoons honey

Place all ingredients in a food processor or blender; process until smooth. Serve immediately over blintzes or yogurt.

SIDE DISHES

BROILED GRAPEFRUIT

4 servings

2 seedless grapefruit, at room
   temperature
2 tablespoons shredded fresh
   coconut
2 tablespoons honey
1 tablespoon finely chopped walnuts
   or pecans
½ teaspoon ground cinnamon

Preheat broiler or oven to 400°F.

Cut the grapefruit in half; use a grapefruit knife to loosen the edges and divide the sections. Place on a baking sheet.

In a small bowl, combine the coconut, honey, nuts, and cinnamon. Spread ¼ of the mixture on each grapefruit half.

Broil the grapefruit halves until they are lightly browned, about 5 minutes, or bake for 10 minutes. Serve warm.

BROILED PINEAPPLE

4 to 6 servings

1 pineapple, cut crosswise into
   slices 1 inch thick
1 tablespoon butter
1 tablespoon honey

Arrange pineapple slices in a single layer in a 9 × 13-inch baking dish.

In a small saucepan, combine the butter and honey; heat. Brush the butter-honey mixture over the pineapple slices.

Place the dish under a broiler, about 5 inches from the heating element. Turn the slices when lightly browned, about 5 minutes. Brush with the butter-honey mixture; brown lightly. Serve immediately.

FRESH FRUIT AMBROSIA

6 servings

6 cups cubed fruits (pineapple,
   strawberries, melon, apples,
   oranges, peaches, seedless
   grapes, blueberries, raspberries)
½ cup shredded fresh coconut
¼ cup raisins
1 egg
¼ cup lemon juice
2 tablespoons honey
2 tablespoons orange juice
½ cup yogurt (page 24)
2 teaspoons grated orange rind
1 teaspoon poppy seeds

In a large bowl, toss the fruit, coconut, and raisins. Refrigerate.

To make the dressing: Lightly beat the egg in a small saucepan. Stir in the lemon juice, honey, and orange juice. Cook over low heat, stirring constantly, until mixture coats the back of a spoon. Cool thoroughly.

Fold in the yogurt, orange rind, and poppy seeds. Chill.

Pour the dressing over individual servings of the fruit.

HONEY-BAKED GINGERED PEARS AND ALMOND STUFFING

6 servings

6 pears
¾ cup almonds
¾ cup raisins
4 tablespoons honey
2 tablespoons butter
½ teaspoon powdered ginger

Preheat oven to 350°F. Generously butter a shallow 6 ×9-inch baking pan.

Core the pears to within ½ inch of the bottoms. Stand them upright in the prepared baking pan.

In a blender or food processor, combine the almonds, raisins, and 2 tablespoons honey. Process until the almonds and raisins are finely chopped but not pureed. Fill the cored pears with this mixture.

In a small saucepan melt together the remaining honey and butter; stir in the ginger. Pour this sauce over the pears.

Bake until the pears are tender when gently pierced with a fork, about 40 minutes. Baste the pears with the ginger sauce several times while baking. Serve hot or chilled.

SUNRISE VEGETABLE SOUP

4 to 6 servings

4 cups tomato juice or mixed vegetable juices
6 tablespoons lemon juice
1 stalk celery, chopped
1 carrot, chopped
1 green pepper, chopped
1 scallion, chopped
½ cucumber, chopped
4 tablespoons chopped fresh parsley
freshly ground pepper, to taste
yogurt (page 24)

In a food processor or blender, process the tomato or vegetable juice and the lemon juice.

Add the celery, carrot, green pepper, scallion, cucumber, and parsley. Puree and chill.

At serving time, top each serving with freshly ground pepper and a dollop of yogurt.

This mixture will keep one week in the refrigerator.

STEWED FRUIT AND YOGURT

6 to 8 servings

1 pound assorted dried fruits
 (prunes, apricots, apples,
 raisins, and pears)
1 orange, thinly sliced
3 cups yogurt (page 24)
½ cup coarsely chopped walnuts

Place the dried fruits in a large saucepan
and cover with water; stir in the orange slices.
Bring to a boil, reduce heat, and simmer until fruit
is well softened, about 1 hour.

To serve, spoon over a scoop of yogurt.
Sprinkle each serving with walnuts.

BREADS

BANANA-APRICOT BREAD

Makes 2 loaves

4 tablespoons poppy seeds
2 cups whole wheat flour
2 teaspoons baking powder
½ teaspoon baking soda
⅔ cup nonfat dry milk
⅓ cup wheat germ
3 eggs, beaten
½ cup safflower oil
½ cup molasses
¼ cup honey
½ teaspoon vanilla extract
3 medium-size bananas, mashed
¾ cup orange juice
½ cup raisins
½ cup chopped dried apricots
½ cup chopped walnuts
½ cup slivered almonds

Preheat oven to 350°F. Oil 2 loaf pans,
9 × 5 inches. Sprinkle each pan with 2 tablespoons poppy seeds; tilt pans to coat bottoms and
sides.

In a large bowl, combine flour, baking
powder, baking soda, dry milk, and wheat germ.

In a separate bowl, combine eggs, oil,
molasses, honey, and vanilla. Add the mashed
bananas and orange juice. Add to the flour
mixture, and stir just until the flour is moistened.
Stir in raisins and apricots. Pour into the loaf
pans. Sprinkle the top of one loaf with the
chopped walnuts, the other with the slivered
almonds.

Bake about 1 hour. The loaves are done
when their centers are firm if pressed lightly with
fingertips. Cool slightly in pans; then, remove
from pans and cool completely on wire racks.

When cool, wrap tightly in foil wrap. The
bread is best when stored in the refrigerator 2 to 3
days before serving. Serve warm with Tangerine-
Cream Cheese (page 33).

CARROT CORN MUFFINS

1 cup whole wheat flour
1 cup cornmeal
2 teaspoons baking powder
3 eggs, beaten
½ cup honey
¼ cup safflower oil
1 cup yogurt (page 24)
1½ cups carrots, grated

Preheat oven to 375°F. Oil enough cups in muffin tins for 16 muffins, or line the cups with paper baking cups.

In a large bowl, mix the flour, cornmeal, and baking powder.

In a small bowl, combine the eggs, honey, and oil; beat in the yogurt.

Add to the flour mixture and stir just until the ingredients are well mixed. Stir in the carrots until evenly distributed.

Pour batter into muffin tins until cups are ⅔ full. Bake about 20 minutes. Serve warm with Maple Butter (page 30).

CRUSTY RYE BREAD

Makes 1 loaf

1 cup milk
1 tablespoon cider vinegar
1 tablespoon honey
3 tablespoons molasses
1½ cups rye flour
¾ cup whole wheat flour
¾ cup wheat germ
½ cup rolled oats
2 tablespoons caraway seeds
1½ teaspoons baking powder
½ teaspoon baking soda

Preheat oven to 350°F. Lightly oil a baking sheet.

In a small bowl, mix milk, vinegar, honey, and molasses.

In a large bowl, combine the rye flour, whole wheat flour, wheat germ, oats, caraway seeds, baking powder, and baking soda. Add the milk mixture and combine well.

Knead the dough on a lightly floured work surface until slightly sticky, 2 to 3 minutes. (If the dough remains very sticky, knead in a little flour.) Shape the dough into a round. Place on the prepared baking sheet. Bake until crusty and well browned, about 1 hour.

Serve warm with Orange Honey (page 32) and butter.

GRANOLA BARS

3 cups Granola (page 33)
2 eggs, beaten
¼ cup orange juice
¼ cup nonfat dry milk
1 teaspoon vanilla extract
½ teaspoon ground nutmeg
½ teaspoon ground cinnamon
1 tablespoon peanut butter
(optional)
1 cup carob chips (optional)
Carob-Peanut Butter Frosting
(optional)

Preheat oven to 350°F. Oil a 9×9-inch baking pan.

In a large bowl, combine the granola, eggs, orange juice, dry milk, vanilla, nutmeg, cinnamon, and peanut butter. Press into the prepared pan.

Sprinkle the carob chips over the top, if desired.

Bake for 20 minutes.

Cool Granola Bars on a wire rack. Frost with the Carob-Peanut Butter Frosting, if desired. Cut into 3-inch square pieces.

IRISH SODA BREAD

3 cups whole wheat flour
1 teaspoon baking soda
4 tablespoons butter
1¼ cups buttermilk
1 tablespoon honey

Preheat oven to 400°F. Oil a baking sheet.

In a large bowl, mix flour and baking soda. Cut in butter with a pastry blender.

In a cup, combine the buttermilk and honey; stir into the flour mixture.

On a lightly floured work surface, knead the dough for 2 minutes. Shape into a flattened, round loaf (about 7 inches in diameter and 1½ inches thick). Place on the prepared baking sheet. With a knife, score an "X" about ¾ inch deep on the top of the loaf.

Bake 25 minutes; reduce heat and bake an additional 20 minutes. Serve with warm Ricotta-Orange Spread (page 32).

ORANGE BRAN MUFFINS

Makes 12 muffins

2 cups bran
½ cup honey
1 cup milk
¼ cup nonfat dry milk
¼ cup orange juice
1 teaspoon grated orange rind
1 egg, beaten
3 tablespoons safflower oil
1 cup whole wheat flour
2 teaspoons baking powder

In a large bowl, mix the bran, honey, milk, dry milk, orange juice, and orange rind. Set aside for 20 minutes.

Preheat oven to 375°F. Oil enough cups in muffin tins for 12 muffins, or line the cups with paper baking cups.

In a small bowl, combine the egg and oil; add to the bran mixture.

In a separate bowl, mix the flour and baking powder. Add the liquid ingredients to this mixture; stir just enough to moisten.

Fill the prepared muffin tins. Bake for 15 to 20 minutes. Serve warm with Strawberry-Honey Butter (page 29).

PEANUT BUTTER-OATMEAL MUFFINS

Makes 12 muffins

1 cup whole wheat flour
1½ teaspoons baking powder
¼ teaspoon powdered mace
1 cup rolled oats
¾ cup milk
1 egg, beaten
⅓ cup chunky peanut butter
⅓ cup honey
¼ cup safflower oil

Preheat oven to 400°F. Oil enough cups in muffin tins for 12 muffins, or line the cups with paper baking cups.

In a large bowl, mix flour, baking powder, and mace. Add oats.

In a separate bowl, combine milk, egg, peanut butter, honey, and oil. Add to the dry ingredients; stir until just moistened.

Spoon mixture into prepared muffin cups. Bake for 20 to 25 minutes. Serve warm with Honey-Butter (page 30) or Banana-Pecan Butter (page 29).

PINEAPPLE-PECAN MUFFINS

Makes 12 muffins

1¼ cups whole wheat flour
½ cup wheat germ, toasted
2 teaspoons baking powder
1 teaspoon baking soda
½ cup butter, at room temperature
½ cup honey
2 eggs
1 cup finely crushed pineapple
1 cup chopped pecans

Preheat oven to 375°F. Oil enough cups in muffin tins for 12 muffins or line the cups with paper baking cups.

In a large bowl, mix the flour, wheat germ, baking powder, and baking soda.

In a separate bowl, cream the butter. Beat in the honey and eggs. Add to the dry ingredients. Stir in the pineapple and pecans.

Spoon into muffin tins. Bake until lightly browned, about 20 minutes.

Lunches
and Picnics

L unch at a friend's home conveys a warmth and hospitality that even the finest restaurant cannot match. The meal can be an informal soup-and-salad snack or an elegant event that features a multi-course menu as the start of a relaxing afternoon. When weather permits, lunches become perfect movable feasts. I like to prepare the food for picnics in advance to avoid makeshift cooking outdoors. With all the clever, inexpensive picnic gadgets and containers on the market, you can easily transport just about any kind of prepared dish — hot, cold, down-home, or gourmet. Festive parties set up in your backyard are also fun. (If it rains, everyone moves to your living room!) Among the delightful picnic dishes in this section are Vegetable-Pasta Salad, Chilled Cucumber Soup, and Tabbouleh in Whole Wheat Pita Bread Pockets.

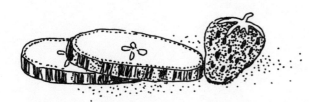

MENUS
LUNCHES AND PICNICS

𝒴 Tabbouleh in Whole Wheat Pita Bread Pockets
   Cucumber-Yogurt Salad
   Cheese-Fruit Spread
   Coconut-Honey Date Bars

𝒴 Vegetarian Chef's Salad with Garden Salad Dressing
   Tofu Bread Sticks
   Fresh Peach Custard Pie with Oatmeal-Wheat Germ Crust

𝒴 Fresh Tomato-Yogurt Soup
   Tofu Salad in Whole Wheat Pita Bread Pockets
   Tropical Fruit Salad
   Carob Chip Cookies

𝒴 Garden Gazpacho
   Date and Wheat Germ Muffins
   Cauliflower-Apple Salad
   Fruit Platter Pie with Whole Wheat Cookie Crust

𝒴 Tomato-Lentil Soup
   Cracked Wheat Bread
   Pecan-Topped Brie
   Spinach Salad with Herbed Tahini Dressing
   Carob-Honey Brownies with Carob-Peanut Butter Frosting

𝒴 Cream of Green Pea-Carrot Soup
   Honey-Pumpkin Muffins
   Marinated Pineapple-Bean Salad
   Sautéed Apple Slices and Orange-Peach Sauce

𝒴 Couscous with Vegetable-Cashew Sauce and Parsley-Egg Sauce
   Kidney Bean-Pineapple Salad
   Maple-Orange Bran Muffins
   Peach Melba with Honey-Raspberry Sauce

Egg Drop Soup
Apricot Muffins
Chinese Vegetable Salad
Kiwi and Papaya Sherbet Duo

Concasse of Tomato
Vegetable-Pasta Salad with Creamy Basil Dressing
Quick Bread Sticks
Carob-Dipped Strawberries
Walnut Torte

Strawberry-Grape Salad with Honey-Mint Dressing
Ratatouille
Nut-Crusted Ricotta Cheesecake with Lemon Glaze

Cheesy Chowder
Walnut-Vegetable Salad
Spicy Carrot Muffins
Strawberry-Rhubarb Pie with Whole Wheat Pastry

Chilled Orange-Yogurt Soup
Indonesian Vegetable Salad and Spicy Peanut Dressing
Banana-Wheat Germ Muffins
Honey Rice Pudding

Zucchini-Ricotta Casserole
Wheat Germ Fried Noodles
Red-Leaf and Asparagus Salad with Creamy French Dressing
Herbed Biscuits
Vanilla-Poached Pears with Honey-Vanilla Custard

Chilled Cucumber Soup
Buttermilk-Whole Wheat Quick Bread
Gateau des Crepes
Asparagus Vinaigrette
White Grape Mousse

MAIN COURSES

CHINESE VEGETABLE SALAD

4 to 6 servings

3 tablespoons cider vinegar
3 tablespoons sesame oil
3 tablespoons soy sauce
1 tablespoon honey
2 tablespoons minced, peeled ginger root
3 drops hot pepper sauce
½ cup safflower oil
2 ounces rice sticks
¾ cup pine nuts
2 cups shredded romaine lettuce
1 cup shredded spinach leaves
2 carrots, cut into matchstick pieces
1 cup bean sprouts
1 cup broccoli florets and stems, cut into matchstick pieces
1 small zucchini, cut into matchstick pieces
1 red sweet pepper, cut into matchstick pieces
1 cup thinly sliced mushrooms
½ pound firm tofu, drained and cut into ¼-inch cubes

In a small bowl, combine vinegar, sesame oil, soy sauce, honey, ginger, and pepper sauce; set aside.

Heat ¼ cup safflower oil in a medium-size skillet over high heat. With tongs, drop in ¼ cup of the rice sticks. Cook until puffed and crisp, 1 to 2 seconds on each side. Remove from pan and drain on paper towels. Repeat with remaining rice sticks. Break apart and set aside.

Heat the remaining ¼ cup safflower oil in the skillet. Add the pine nuts, and stir until lightly browned. Remove with a slotted spoon and drain on paper towels. Set aside.

In a large salad bowl, toss the romaine, spinach, carrots, sprouts, broccoli, zucchini, pepper, and mushrooms. Gently toss in tofu, rice sticks, and pine nuts.

Just before serving, add the dressing and toss again. Serve the salad on a large platter.

COUSCOUS WITH VEGETABLE-CASHEW SAUCE AND PARSLEY-EGG SAUCE

6 servings

2 cups dry couscous
2 cups Vegetable Stock (page 35), heated
Vegetable-Cashew Sauce (see accompanying recipe)
Parsley-Egg Sauce (see accompanying recipe)

Mix the couscous and stock. Let stand covered until liquid is completely absorbed, 5 to 10 minutes. Toss lightly.

Serve immediately with Vegetable-Cashew Sauce and Parsley-Egg Sauce.

Vegetable-Cashew Sauce

Yields about 1½ cups

2 tablespoons butter
1 clove garlic, minced
1 medium-size onion, chopped
2 medium-size tomatoes, cubed
1 medium-size green pepper, diced
1 medium-size zucchini, cubed
2 carrots, sliced
½ cup raw cashews
1 tablespoon lemon juice
1 teaspoon dried basil
1 teaspoon dried oregano
½ teaspoon rosemary
¼ teaspoon pepper
8 large mushrooms, sliced
½ cup golden raisins
2 hard-cooked eggs, minced

Melt butter in medium-size saucepan; add garlic and onion; cook until tender. Add tomatoes, green pepper, zucchini, carrots, cashews, lemon juice, basil, oregano, rosemary, and pepper. Cover and cook over low heat 15 minutes. Add mushrooms and raisins. Cover and cook until all vegetables are tender, 5 to 10 minutes.

Serve hot over couscous; garnish each serving with hard-cooked eggs.

Vegetable-Cashew Sauce may also be used as a filling in omelets or as a sauce over baked potatoes.

Parsley-Egg Sauce

Yields 1½ cups

2 hard-cooked eggs
1½ cups milk
3 tablespoons butter
3 tablespoons whole wheat flour
2 tablespoons minced fresh parsley
¼ teaspoon dry mustard
2 teaspoons soy sauce
dash of garlic powder
white pepper, to taste
paprika

In a blender or food processor process the eggs and milk until smooth; set aside.

In a medium-size saucepan, melt the butter; stir in the flour. Reduce heat and cook, stirring constantly, for 1 minute. Stir in the egg-and-milk mixture. Add the remaining ingredients, except paprika, and heat through.

Serve hot over couscous; sprinkle paprika on each serving.

This sauce is also excellent when served on steamed vegetables.

GATEAU DES CREPES

Whole Wheat Crepes (see
  accompanying recipe)
Bechamel Sauce (see
  accompanying recipe)
Spinach Filling (see
  accompanying recipe)
Mushroom Filling (see
  accompanying recipe)
3 tablespoons grated Parmesan
  cheese
¼ cup sliced almonds
  paprika

Prepare Whole Wheat Crepes, Bechamel Sauce, Spinach Filling, and Mushroom Filling according to recipes.

Preheat oven to 350°F. Butter a round 9-inch baking dish.

Place a crepe in the bottom of the baking dish. Spread on it a layer of Mushroom Filling. Place a crepe on top and spread a layer of Spinach Filling on it. Continue alternating layers of crepes and fillings, ending with a crepe.

Pour the Bechamel Sauce over the top and sides of the Gateau, and sprinkle it with Parmesan. Bake to heat through and lightly brown the top, 25 to 30 minutes. Garnish with almond slices and paprika. To serve, cut into wedges.

If you wish to prepare this recipe in advance, make the crepes, fillings, and sauce; refrigerate separately. Assemble and bake the Gateau just before serving.

Whole Wheat Crepes

Makes 10 crepes

1 cup whole wheat flour
1¾ cups milk
¼ cup cold water
2 eggs
1 tablespoon safflower oil

Place all ingredients in a food processor or blender and process until smooth. Cover and refrigerate 2 hours.

Lightly oil a 7-inch crepe pan; heat over high heat. Remove from heat and pour a scant ¼ cup of batter into the middle of the pan. Tilt the pan so that the batter covers the bottom; pour off the excess. Return the pan to the heat for about 1 minute. When the edges of the crepe begin to pull away from the pan, flip the crepe and lightly brown the other side for about ½ minute. Remove crepe from pan to cool.

Repeat this procedure with the remaining batter.

Bechamel Sauce

Yields about 1 cup

1 tablespoon butter
1 tablespoon whole wheat flour
¾ cup milk
⅛ teaspoon pepper
    dash of ground nutmeg
¼ cup grated cheddar or Swiss
    cheese (1 ounce)

In a saucepan, melt the butter; add the flour and stir over medium heat until bubbly. Remove from heat and stir in the milk. Cook, stirring constantly, until the sauce is smooth and thick. Add the pepper, nutmeg, and cheese; continue stirring over low heat until the cheese has melted. Set aside.

Spinach Filling

Yields about 1 cup

2 tablespoons butter
1 scallion, minced
½ cup cooked spinach, drained
¼ cup sliced almonds
½ teaspoon ground nutmeg
    dash of pepper
½ cup Cottage Cheese Sauce (see
    accompanying recipe)

In a small saucepan, melt the butter; stir in the scallion and sauté until softened. Squeeze moisture from spinach, then add to the scallions. Add the almonds, nutmeg, and pepper.

Stir over high heat for about 3 minutes. Remove from heat; stir in the Cottage Cheese Sauce. Set aside.

Mushroom Filling

Yields about ¾ cup

2 tablespoons butter
8 ounces mushrooms, chopped
2 scallions, minced
    dash of pepper
½ cup Cottage Cheese Sauce (see
    accompanying recipe)

In a small skillet, melt the butter; sauté the mushrooms and scallions until softened. Drain if necessary and add the pepper. Stir in the Cottage Cheese Sauce. Set aside.

Cottage Cheese Sauce

Yields 1 cup

1 cup cottage cheese (8 ounces)
1 egg

Puree the cottage cheese and egg in a food processor or blender.

INDONESIAN VEGETABLE SALAD AND SPICY PEANUT DRESSING

4 to 6 servings

6 tablespoons safflower oil
¼ cup finely chopped onions
1 clove garlic, minced
1 cup water
juice of 1 lemon
½ cup smooth peanut butter
1 tablespoon cider vinegar
1 tablespoon honey
1 tablespoon soy sauce
1 teaspoon chili powder
cayenne pepper, to taste
1 cup cubed, drained, firm tofu
2 cups cut green beans, steamed and cooled
2 stalks celery, cut into julienne strips
2 carrots, cut into julienne strips
2 cups shredded cabbage
2 tomatoes, cut into thin wedges
1 cup bean sprouts
1 cucumber, thinly sliced
1 cup broccoli florets
1 cup cauliflower florets
12 to 16 leaves spinach
12 to 16 leaves Boston lettuce
4 hard-cooked eggs, cut into wedges
½ cup raisins
¼ cup sesame seeds

To make the peanut dressing: Heat 4 tablespoons oil in a medium-size skillet; sauté onions and garlic until limp. Add water, lemon juice, peanut butter, vinegar, honey, soy sauce, chili powder, and cayenne; simmer 1 minute. Chill.

Heat the remaining 2 tablespoons oil in the skillet. Add tofu and fry until lightly browned. Drain and set aside to cool.

To assemble the salad: Line plates with spinach and lettuce leaves. Arrange the vegetables and egg wedges attractively on each plate. Spoon Spicy Peanut Dressing over each salad; garnish with raisins and sesame seeds. Serve immediately.

RATATOUILLE

⅓ cup safflower oil
1 medium-size onion, quartered and
   sliced
2 cloves garlic, minced
2 medium-size green peppers, sliced
2 medium-size zucchini, cut in
   julienne strips
1 small eggplant, cut in julienne
   strips
2 cups green beans, cut in ½-inch
   lengths and steamed
¾ cup raw cashews, chopped
4 tablespoons cider vinegar
2½ cups tomato sauce
1 tablespoon honey
1 teaspoon dried basil
1 teaspoon dried oregano
1 teaspoon pepper
3 medium-size tomatoes, cubed
6 whole wheat pita bread pockets
2 cups alfalfa sprouts

In a Dutch oven or large heavy saucepan, heat oil; sauté onion until glossy. Add garlic, green pepper, zucchini, eggplant, green beans, and cashews. Spinkle vinegar over vegetables. Cook 10 minutes over medium heat, stirring occasionally.

Add tomato sauce, honey, basil, oregano, and pepper. Cover and simmer over low heat, 30 to 40 minutes, stirring occasionally.

Remove from heat. Add tomatoes to mixture, and stir gently. Let stand, covered, in a warm place for 1 hour. Chill.

Serve in whole wheat pita bread pockets, and garnish each serving with alfalfa sprouts.

Ratatouille is also tasty when served warm, and it makes an excellent filling for omelets and crepes, or as a topping for baked potatoes garnished with melted cheese.

TABBOULEH IN WHOLE WHEAT PITA BREAD POCKETS

6 to 8 servings

2 cups boiling water or Vegetable
    Stock (page 35)
1 cup bulgur
3 stalks celery, chopped
½ cup chopped scallions
½ cup cooked chick-peas, drained
2 medium-size tomatoes, cut into
    ½-inch cubes
1 cup minced fresh parsley
½ cup lemon juice
¼ cup safflower or olive oil
2 teaspoons dried mint or ¼ cup
    chopped fresh mint
¼ teaspoon pepper
    dash of ground cinnamon
    dash of ground allspice
    dash of ground nutmeg
6 whole wheat pita bread pockets
    alfalfa sprouts

In a large bowl, pour boiling water or stock over the bulgur.

Soak until bulgur is softened, about ½ hour. Drain off any unabsorbed liquid.

Toss the remaining ingredients, except the pita bread and sprouts, with the bulgur. Cover and refrigerate several hours or overnight to allow flavors to blend.

To serve, stuff the mixture into pita bread pockets and garnish with alfalfa sprouts.

Tabbouleh may also be served on lettuce or spinach leaves as a salad. For variety, add other beans, sunflower seeds, chopped hard-cooked eggs, or other chopped or sliced vegetables such as cucumbers, zucchini, avocado, or mushrooms.

Or, substitute cracked wheat for the bulgur. To prepare cracked wheat, boil it about 5 minutes, then soak, in the same way as the bulgur.

TOFU SALAD IN WHOLE WHEAT PITA BREAD POCKETS

8 servings

1 pound firm tofu, drained
3 tablespoons yogurt (page 24) or
    Mayonnaise (page 31)
1 stalk celery, chopped
1 carrot, chopped
¼ green pepper, chopped
2 tablespoons minced scallions
1 tablespoon Mustard (page 31)
½ teaspoon soy sauce
½ teaspoon tumeric
¼ teaspoon pepper
⅛ teaspoon garlic powder
    dash of ground cumin
8 whole wheat pita bread pockets
    alfalfa sprouts
2 tomatoes, cut into 16 wedges

Mash tofu with a fork. Add the remaining ingredients, except the pita bread pockets, sprouts, and tomato wedges. Mix thoroughly.

Stuff pita pockets with the salad; then, top with alfalfa sprouts and tomato wedges.

This salad also makes a tasty filling for tomato shells. To make the shells, remove the tops from 8 tomatoes and scoop out the centers. Fill with the salad and garnish with sprouts or parsley sprigs. Serve on a bed of Boston lettuce.

For special party hors d'oeuvres, spread the salad on whole grain crackers and top each with half a cherry tomato and a small parsley sprig.

VEGETARIAN CHEF'S SALAD WITH GARDEN SALAD DRESSING

6 servings

 1 head romaine lettuce, shredded
1½ cups broccoli florets
 1 cup cauliflower florets
 1 cup cut green beans, steamed and chilled
 6 new potatoes, cooked, chilled, and cut into 1-inch cubes
12 cherry tomatoes
 2 carrots, sliced
 1 stalk celery, sliced
 ½ green pepper, chopped
 ¼ cup chopped scallions
 2 hard-cooked eggs, chopped or sliced
 2 apples, chopped
 ½ orange, chopped
 1 cup raisins
 ½ cup chopped walnuts
 1 cup cubed colby cheese (4 ounces)
 1 cup cubed Monterey Jack cheese (4 ounces)
 4 tablespoons sesame seeds
 4 tablespoons sunflower seeds
    freshly ground pepper, to taste
    wheat germ
    Garden Salad Dressing (see following recipe)

In a large salad bowl, combine all the ingredients except the pepper, wheat germ, and salad dressing. Toss well.

Mound on chilled plates; sprinkle pepper and wheat germ on each serving. Serve with Garden Salad Dressing.

Garden Salad Dressing

Yields 3 cups

 2 carrots, cut into chunks
 2 scallions, cut into chunks
 2 stalks celery, cut into chunks
 3 sprigs of parsley
 2 cloves garlic
 ¾ teaspoon dry mustard
 ½ teaspoon pepper
 6 tablespoons cider vinegar
 2 eggs
 1 cup safflower oil

Place all ingredients except oil in food processor or blender; process until pureed. Continue to blend, gradually adding oil.

Chill several hours or overnight before serving as a salad dressing or a dip for fresh vegetables.

VEGETABLE-PASTA SALAD WITH
CREAMY BASIL DRESSING

6 servings

8 ounces uncooked whole wheat
    spaghetti
2 tablespoons olive oil
2 cloves garlic, minced
1 cup shredded mozzarella cheese
    (4 ounces)
2 cups chopped broccoli florets,
    steamed
2 cups chick-peas, cooked
2 cups cherry tomatoes, cut in
    halves
2 cups peas, cooked
8 ounces mushrooms, sliced
1 red sweet pepper, cut into strips
1 cup chopped celery
1 6-ounce jar artichoke hearts,
    drained
3 scallions, chopped
1 pound spinach leaves
2 cups Creamy Basil Dressing (see
    following recipe)
    freshly ground pepper, to taste
1 cup watercress leaves
1 cup chopped walnuts
    freshly grated Parmesan cheese

Fill a 3-quart saucepan with water and heat to a boil; add spaghetti. Let water return to a boil; reduce heat and cook spaghetti until just tender, 8 to 10 minutes. Do not overcook! Drain in a colander and return the pasta to the empty pot. Toss with the oil and garlic. Add the mozzarella and toss over low heat until the cheese is melted and evenly distributed, about 5 minutes. Add the vegetables except spinach and toss to mix thoroughly.

Refrigerate the pasta salad until ready to serve.

To serve: Arrange spinach leaves around the outer edges of chilled plates. Place a mound of pasta salad on each plate; spoon a generous portion of Creamy Basil Dressing on each serving; sprinkle with freshly ground pepper. Garnish with watercress leaves and chopped walnuts. Serve with the Parmesan.

Creamy Basil Dressing

Yields 2 cups

6 tablespoons cider vinegar
3 tablespoons chopped fresh basil
2 tablespoons Mustard (page 31)
2 large cloves garlic, minced
6 tablespoons safflower oil
1½ cups yogurt (page 24)
    freshly ground pepper, to taste

Place the vinegar, basil, mustard, and garlic in a food processor or blender; process until almost smooth. With the machine running continuously, gradually add the oil. Stir in the yogurt, and season with pepper. Cover and refrigerate. Stir well before serving.

This dressing is most flavorful when allowed to mellow for a day.

ZUCCHINI-RICOTTA CASSEROLE

6 to 8 servings

 1 28-ounce can whole peeled Italian
   plum tomatoes
 2 tablespoons butter
 1 tablespoon safflower oil
 1 tablespoon olive oil
 3 medium-size zucchini, sliced
   ¼-inch thick
 1 medium-size onion, minced
 1 clove garlic, minced
 1 teaspoon dried basil
   pinch of ground nutmeg
   pepper, to taste
 2 eggs, beaten
 1 cup ricotta cheese (8 ounces)
 1 cup heavy cream
 1 cup freshly grated Parmesan
   cheese (4 ounces)

Preheat oven to 450°F. Oil a 2-quart baking dish. Drain the tomatoes; cut into quarters.

In a large skillet, over medium heat, warm the butter, the safflower oil, and the olive oil. Add the zucchini and cook, stirring constantly, until crisp-tender. Remove the zucchini and drain.

Add the onion to the skillet and cook over medium heat until tender. Stir in the garlic, basil nutmeg, pepper, and tomatoes. Cook until most of the moisture evaporates, 8 to 10 minutes.

In a medium-size bowl, combine the eggs, ricotta, cream, and Parmesan cheese.

Arrange half the zucchini in the bottom of the prepared baking dish; spread the tomato mixture on top. Next, arrange a layer of the remaining zucchini; top with the ricotta cheese mixture.

Bake for 15 minutes. Reduce the oven temperature to 375°F and continue baking until the top is browned and slightly puffed, about 25 minutes. Let stand 5 minutes before serving.

SALADS

CAULIFLOWER-APPLE SALAD

6 servings

 2 unpeeled red apples, cut into ½
   inch cubes
 3 tablespoons lemon juice
 3 cups cauliflower florets
 1 cup cubed cheddar cheese
   (4 ounces)
 ½ cup chopped pecans
 ½ cup yogurt (page 24)
 1 tablespoon Mayonnaise (page 31)
 1 tablespoon Mustard (page 31)
 1 tablespoon honey
 ¼ teaspoon paprika

Place the apple cubes in a large bowl. Drizzle with 2 tablespoons of the lemon juice. Add the cauliflower, cheese cubes, and pecans; toss.

In a small bowl, combine the remaining ingredients. Pour over the cauliflower-apple mixture and gently toss.

This recipe looks and tastes best when served shortly after preparation.

CUCUMBER-YOGURT SALAD

4 to 6 servings

2 cucumbers, seeded, and cut into
   julienne strips
2 teaspoons lemon juice
½ cup yogurt (page 24)
1 clove garlic, minced
2 tablespoons chopped fresh mint
¼ cup chopped fresh parsley
¾ teaspoon pepper
½ teaspoon dillweed

Place the cucumber strips in a medium-size bowl. Add the lemon juice and mix well. Stir in the remaining ingredients. Chill several hours before serving.

KIDNEY BEAN-PINEAPPLE SALAD

6 servings

2 cups cooked kidney beans
2 scallions, chopped
2 stalks celery, chopped
1 cup chopped pineapple
½ cup cubed cheddar cheese
   (2 ounces)
3 tablespoons cider vinegar
2 tablespoons safflower or corn oil
2 tablespoons Mayonnaise (page 31)
2 tablespoons yogurt (page 24)
¼ teaspoon dillweed
¼ teaspoon ground coriander
   freshly ground pepper, to taste
12 large leaves spinach or 6 leaves
   romaine lettuce

In a large bowl, toss the kidney beans, scallions, celery, pineapple, and cheese.

In a small bowl, combine the vinegar, oil, mayonnaise, yogurt, dill, coriander, and pepper. Pour over the salad ingredients, toss gently.

Cover and refrigerate at least 1 hour before serving.

Serve mounds of salad on beds of spinach or romaine leaves.

MARINATED PINEAPPLE-BEAN SALAD

6 to 8 servings

  1 cup chopped pineapple, drained
1½ cups cooked red kidney beans,
       drained
  ¼ cup minced sweet red onion
  2 tablespoons chopped fresh parsley
  ⅓ cup lemon juice
  ⅓ cup safflower oil
  2 cloves garlic, minced
  ½ teaspoon dried thyme leaves
  ¼ teaspoon ground coriander
       dash of ground cumin
       freshly ground pepper, to taste
  1 tomato, cut into ½-inch cubes
  ½ cup cubed cheddar or colby
       cheese (2 ounces)
  1 head Bibb lettuce

In a medium-size bowl, toss pineapple, beans, onion, and parsley.

In a small bowl, combine lemon juice, oil, garlic, thyme, coriander, cumin, and pepper. Pour over the fruit-and-bean mixture. Cover and marinate at least 4 hours before serving.

When ready to serve, stir in tomato cubes and cheese cubes. Serve on beds of lettuce.

RED-LEAF AND ASPARAGUS SALAD WITH CREAMY FRENCH DRESSING

6 servings

  2 bunches red-leaf lettuce, torn
18 spears asparagus, steamed and
       chilled
       Creamy French Dressing (see
       following recipe)
  3 hard-cooked eggs, finely chopped

For each serving, place 3 asparagus spears on a bed of red-leaf lettuce. Pour on Creamy French Dressing; garnish with chopped eggs.

Creamy French Dressing

Yields 1⅔ cups

  1 teaspoon honey
  1 tablespoon paprika
       pinch of cayenne pepper
  ⅓ cup cider vinegar
  1 egg
  ⅔ cup safflower oil

In a small bowl, combine honey, paprika, and cayenne; then add vinegar and egg. Beat well. Add oil gradually, beating constantly.

SPINACH SALAD WITH HERBED TAHINI DRESSING

6 servings

1 pound spinach, stems removed
3 hard-cooked eggs, minced
1 cup sliced mushrooms
⅓ cup sesame seeds
1 cup alfalfa sprouts
  Herbed Tahini Dressing (see following recipe)

Toss together all ingredients except sprouts and dressing. Sprinkle sprouts over top. Chill. Serve with Herbed Tahini Dressing.

Herbed Tahini Dressing

Yields about 1¼ cups

1 cup yogurt (page 24)
2 cloves garlic, minced
2 tablespoons chopped fresh parsley
3 tablespoons tahini (sesame butter)
1 tablespoon safflower oil
1 tablespoon chopped chives
1 teaspoon lemon juice
2 teaspoons honey
½ teaspoon grated lemon rind
½ teaspoon pepper

Put all ingredients in a food processor or blender, and process until smooth.

TROPICAL FRUIT SALAD

6 servings

1 papaya, cut into 1-inch cubes
1 avocado, cut into 1-inch cubes
¼ cup lemon juice
¼ teaspoon ground coriander
¼ teaspoon ground allspice
  dash of white pepper
1 cup watercress leaves

In a large bowl, combine papaya and avocado.

In a small bowl, combine lemon juice, coriander, allspice, and white pepper. Pour this dressing over the fruit mixture and toss lightly. Cover and refrigerate 1 to 2 hours.

At serving time toss in the watercress.

STRAWBERRY-GRAPE SALAD WITH HONEY-MINT DRESSING

6 servings

1 large head romaine lettuce
1 pint fresh strawberries
1 cup seedless white grapes
¼ cup coarsely chopped walnuts or slivered almonds
½ cup Honey-Mint Dressing (see following recipe)

Tear lettuce leaves into bite-size pieces and place in a large salad bowl. Toss with remaining ingredients except dressing. Chill. Just before serving, add Honey-Mint Dressing and toss. Serve with additional dressing.

Honey-Mint Dressing

Yields about 1 cup

⅔ cup olive or safflower oil
¼ cup honey
¼ cup cider vinegar
3 cloves garlic, speared on toothpicks
2 tablespoons dried mint leaves or 2 sprigs of mint, leaves chopped
½ teaspoon freshly ground pepper

Combine all ingredients and let stand 3 hours at room temperature. Remove garlic. Serve on Strawberry-Grape Salad.

WALNUT-VEGETABLE SALAD

6 servings

2 medium-size cucumbers, thinly sliced
2 medium-size tomatoes, cubed
3 stalks celery, very thinly sliced
1 cup walnuts
2 cloves garlic, minced
    dash of cayenne pepper
2 tablespoons cider vinegar
6 tablespoons cold water
4 tablespoons lemon juice
4 tablespoons chopped fresh parsley
2 tablespoons minced onion
1 teaspoon ground coriander
6 large leaves romaine or 12 large leaves spinach
    sprigs of parsley

In a large bowl, combine the cucumbers, tomatoes, and celery. Set aside and chill.

In a food processor or blender, process the walnuts, garlic, and cayenne to a paste. Add the vinegar, water, and lemon juice; blend until smooth. Stir in the parsley, onion, and coriander. Pour this sauce over the chilled vegetables and mix gently but thoroughly.

To serve, place mounds of the salad on beds of romaine or spinach leaves; garnish with parsley sprigs.

SOUPS

CHEESY CHOWDER

6 servings

¼ cup butter
1 medium-size potato, cut into
    ½-inch cubes
1 carrot, chopped
1 stalk celery, chopped
1 medium-size onion, chopped
½ green pepper, chopped
3 cups Vegetable Stock (page 35)
    dash of pepper
2 cups milk
¼ cup nonfat dry milk
½ cup whole wheat pastry flour
3 cups shredded cheddar cheese
    (12 ounces)
1 tablespoon chopped fresh parsley
    paprika

In a 2-quart saucepan, melt the butter. Stir in the potato, carrot, celery, onion, and green pepper; cook until tender but not brown, about 10 minutes. Add the stock and pepper. Bring to a boil; reduce heat, cover, and simmer for 30 minutes.

In a large bowl, combine the milk and dry milk; stir until the milk powder has dissolved. Add the flour; then stir in the cheese. Stir this mixture into the chowder; cook, stirring constantly, until the soup is thick and smooth, about 5 minutes. Stir in the parsley. Top each serving with a dash of paprika.

CHILLED CUCUMBER SOUP

6 servings

1 large cucumber
2 tablespoons safflower oil
1 stalk celery, chopped
1 small onion, chopped
1 clove garlic, minced
1½ teaspoons curry powder
    dash of white pepper
3 cups Vegetable Stock (page 35)
1½ cups yogurt (page 24)
3 tablespoons chopped fresh parsley
    or dillweed

Cut 6 thin slices from the cucumber and reserve for garnish. Coarsely chop the remaining cucumber.

Heat the oil in a large saucepan. Sauté the chopped cucumber, celery, onion, and garlic until tender. Sprinkle with curry and pepper. Add stock; cover and simmer about 30 minutes.

Pour the mixture into a food processor or blender, and puree. Add the yogurt and blend thoroughly. Chill for several hours.

Serve chilled or warm, and garnish each serving with a cucumber slice and a sprinkling of parsley or dill.

CHILLED ORANGE-YOGURT SOUP

4 to 6 servings

2 cups orange juice
2 cups pineapple juice
3 whole cloves
2 tablespoons honey
2 tablespoons cornstarch
¼ cup lemon juice
¼ teaspoon ground cinnamon
1 cup yogurt (page 24)
1 orange, cubed
¼ cup almond slices

In a medium-size saucepan, mix the orange juice and pineapple juice with the whole cloves. Bring to boil; simmer 10 minutes; remove the cloves.

In a cup, mix the honey and cornstarch. Add to the boiling juices and cook until slightly thick, about 2 minutes. Cool. Stir in the lemon juice and cinnamon. Chill the mixture thoroughly.

Before serving, stir in the yogurt and orange. Garnish each serving with about 1 tablespoon of almond slices.

CONCASSE OF TOMATO

6 servings

6 medium-size tomatoes, peeled and diced
2 cups tomato juice
3 scallions, minced
2 tablespoons minced fresh parsley
1 tablespoon chopped fresh basil
1 tablespoon dried oregano
2 tablespoons lemon juice
4 tablespoons olive oil
6 tablespoons minced mushrooms
6 tablespoons minced zucchini
   freshly ground pepper, to taste

In a large bowl, combine all ingredients except mushrooms, zucchini, and pepper. Chill.

To serve: Garnish each serving with chopped mushrooms, chopped zucchini, and a grating of pepper.

CREAM OF GREEN PEA-CARROT SOUP

6 to 8 servings

1½ cups water
2 pounds peas, shelled, or 6 cups frozen peas
¼ cup chopped onion
¼ teaspoon white pepper
1 tablespoon honey
2 tablespoons whole wheat flour
2 cups milk or light cream
¼ teaspoon ground nutmeg
2 cups sliced carrots, steamed until crisp-tender
¾ cup yogurt (page 24)

In a large saucepan or Dutch oven, bring the water to a boil. Add the peas, onion, pepper, and honey. Return to a boil; reduce heat to low, cover, and cook for 20 minutes.

Pour 2 cups of the water-and-pea mixture into a food processor or blender. Process until smooth. Pour into a large bowl or saucepan and set aside. Puree another 2 cups of the mixture. Repeat the steps until all the mixture has been pureed. (The puree may be stored up to 2 days, if desired.)

When ready to serve the soup, pour the pureed mixture into a saucepan and heat slowly over low heat.

In a small bowl, mix the flour, milk, and nutmeg; stir until smooth. Add this mixture to the warmed soup. Increase heat to medium and stir constantly until mixture just reaches the boiling point, but be careful not to boil.

Stir in the carrot slices and continue to heat the mixture for 5 minutes over low heat. Taste for seasonings and consistency. For a thinner soup, add more milk.

Ladle into soup bowls; garnish each serving with a dollop of yogurt; serve immediately.

EGG DROP SOUP

6 servings

6 cups Vegetable Stock (page 35)
2 tablespoons minced scallions
2 teaspoons sesame oil
2 teaspoons soy sauce
dash of white pepper
1 cup peas
4 eggs, beaten

Pour the stock into a large saucepan. Stir in scallions, sesame oil, soy sauce, and pepper. Bring the liquid to a boil. Add the peas, cover, and cook 5 minutes.

While the soup cooks, add the eggs by pouring slowly in a very thin stream. Continue stirring until the eggs cook and form shreds. Serve immediately.

FRESH TOMATO-YOGURT SOUP

4 to 6 servings

5 medium-size tomatoes, peeled,
    seeded, and chopped
2½ cups yogurt (page 24)
1 clove garlic, crushed
½ teaspoon curry powder
    juice of 1 lemon
    freshly ground pepper, to taste
1 tablespoon honey (optional)
2 tablespoons minced fresh parsley

Puree tomatoes in food processor or blender. (The tomatoes should yield about 2½ cups of puree.) Stir in 2 cups yogurt, garlic, curry powder, lemon juice, and pepper. Taste; then add honey if the mixture is too tart. Refrigerate for several hours.

Serve in chilled bowls; garnish each serving with a dollop of yogurt and a sprinkling of parsley.

GARDEN GAZPACHO

4 to 6 servings

1½ cups (15-ounce can) tomato sauce
1 teaspoon honey
¼ cup (2-ounce jar) chopped
    pimiento
1 medium-size green pepper,
    chopped
1 medium-size tomato, cubed
½ cucumber, seeded and cubed
2 tablespoons safflower oil
2 tablespoons cider vinegar
    freshly ground pepper, to taste
    hot pepper sauce, to taste
1 clove garlic

In a medium-size bowl, combine tomato sauce and honey. Stir in pimiento, green pepper, tomato, cucumber, oil, vinegar, pepper, and pepper sauce. Spear the garlic on a toothpick and place in the soup mixture. Cover and chill for several hours or overnight.

To serve, remove garlic, pour into chilled bowls, and garnish each serving with Seasoned Whole Wheat Croutons (page 34).

TOMATO-LENTIL SOUP

6 servings

⅔ cup dried lentils
4 cups Vegetable Stock (page 35)
   or water
1 tablespoon butter
2 cloves garlic, minced
1 medium-size onion, chopped
4 carrots, chopped
2 stalks celery, chopped
3 cups (28-ounce can) cooked
   tomatoes
1 bay leaf
¾ cup (6-ounce can) tomato paste
¼ cup chopped fresh parsley
1 teaspoon dried thyme leaves
1 teaspoon dillweed
1 teaspoon dried tarragon
1 teaspoon dried marjoram
   freshly ground pepper, to taste

Sort and rinse the lentils. In a Dutch oven or large saucepan, combine the lentils and stock or water.

In a large skillet, melt the butter over low heat. Sauté the garlic and onion until onion is tender but not brown. Add to the lentils and stock. Stir in the carrots, celery, tomatoes, and bay leaf. Simmer gently about 1 hour.

In a cup, combine the tomato paste, parsley, thyme, dillweed, tarragon, and marjoram. Remove the bay leaf from the soup; stir in the tomato paste mixture. Heat; add pepper to taste.

Serve piping hot.

SIDE DISHES

ASPARAGUS VINAIGRETTE

6 servings

½ cup safflower oil
3 tablespoons cider vinegar
½ teaspoon honey
½ teaspoon dry mustard
¼ teaspoon white pepper
⅛ teaspoon garlic powder
   dash of paprika
   dash of hot pepper sauce
2 pounds asparagus spears,
   steamed until crisp-tender
6 cherry tomatoes
2 hard-cooked eggs, minced
   rind of 1 lemon, coarsely grated

Make the vinaigrette sauce by combining the oil, vinegar, honey, mustard, pepper, garlic, paprika, and pepper sauce. Pour over the asparagus; cover and refrigerate.

To serve, garnish each serving with a cherry tomato and 1 tablespoon of the egg. Top with lemon rind.

CHEESE-FRUIT SPREAD

Yields about 2 cups

8 ounces kefir cheese or cream
   cheese, softened
2 cups shredded cheddar cheese
   (8 ounces)
¼ cup finely chopped dried apricots
¼ cup finely chopped dates
1 teaspoon ground coriander
   dash of soy sauce
½ cup chopped pecans

In a food processor or blender, process kefir or cream cheese and cheddar cheese until smooth. Stir in apricots, dates, coriander, and soy sauce. Spoon into medium-size serving bowl; chill at least 4 hours before serving to allow fruit to soften.

Before serving, top with chopped pecans. Serve with crackers or whole wheat pita bread pockets.

PECAN-TOPPED BRIE

6 servings

8 ounces whole Brie cheese
2 teaspoons butter, melted
¼ cup pecan halves
2 apples, cut into wedges
2 pears, cut into wedges

Place Brie in a 6-inch round baking dish; brush with melted butter. Arrange pecan halves decoratively on top. Bake in 350°F oven just until cheese begins to melt, 10 to 15 minutes. To serve, scoop up with apple or pear wedges, or spread on slices of bread.

WHEAT GERM FRIED NOODLES

6 servings

3 cups spinach noodles
4 tablespoons butter
¾ cup toasted wheat germ
   dash of pepper

Place noodles and 1 tablespoon butter in a large pot of boiling water; reduce heat and cook until noodles are tender, about 5 minutes. Drain and dry on paper towels.

Melt remaining butter in a large skillet. Over medium heat, fry the noodles until lightly browned. Stir in the wheat germ and pepper. Serve immediately.

BREADS

APRICOT MUFFINS

Makes 24 muffins

1 cup chopped dried apricots
3 cups whole wheat flour
1 tablespoon baking powder
1 teaspoon ground cinnamon
¼ teaspoon ground nutmeg
1¼ cups milk
1 cup honey
1 egg, beaten
3 tablespoons safflower oil
1 cup chopped pecans or almonds

Place apricot pieces in a small bowl. Add hot water to cover; let stand until fruit is softened, about 30 minutes. Drain well.

Preheat oven to 375°F. Oil enough cups in muffin tins for 24 muffins or line cups with paper baking cups.

In a large bowl, mix the flour, baking powder, cinnamon, and nutmeg.

In a separate bowl, combine the milk, honey, egg, and oil. Add to the flour mixture; stir only until the flour is thoroughly moistened. Gently fold in the apricots and pecans or almonds.

Spoon into the muffin tins, and bake about 20 minutes. Serve warm with Honey Butter (page 30), Orange-Honey Butter (page 29), or Orange Pineapple Butter (page 29).

BANANA-WHEAT GERM MUFFINS

Makes 12 muffins

¾ cup whole wheat flour
¼ cup toasted wheat germ
1 teaspoon baking powder
½ teaspoon baking soda
¼ cup butter, at room temperature
½ cup honey
1 egg, beaten
2 tablespoons orange juice
½ teaspoon vanilla extract
1 banana, mashed
½ cup chopped walnuts
1 tablespoon orange rind

Preheat oven to 375°F. Oil enough cups in muffin tins for 12 muffins or line the cups with paper baking cups.

In a large bowl mix the flour, wheat germ, baking powder, and baking soda.

In a separate small bowl, cream the butter. Beat in the honey, egg, orange juice, and vanilla. Add to the dry ingredients. Stir in the banana, walnuts, and orange rind.

Spoon into the muffin tins and bake until lightly browned, 15 to 20 minutes.

BUTTERMILK-WHOLE WHEAT QUICK BREAD

Makes 2 loaves

¼ cup poppy seeds
2 cups whole wheat flour
¼ cup soy flour
¼ cup bran
¼ cup wheat germ
¼ cup nonfat dry milk
1 teaspoon baking soda
1 teaspoon baking powder
¼ cup sesame seeds
1 cup buttermilk
1 cup milk
¼ cup maple syrup
2 tablespoons safflower oil
1 tablespoon molasses
1 egg, beaten
4 tablespoons rolled oats

Preheat oven to 350°F. Oil 2 loaf pans, 4 ×8 inches. Sprinkle the bottom and sides of each pan with 2 tablespoons of poppy seeds.

In a large bowl, combine the whole wheat flour, soy flour, wheat germ, dry milk, baking soda, baking powder, and sesame seeds.

In a medium-size bowl, combine the buttermilk, milk, syrup, oil, molasses, and egg. Add to the dry ingredients; stir just until moistened.

Pour batter into the loaf pans. Sprinkle each loaf with 2 tablespoons rolled oats.

Bake until tester inserted in center comes out clean, about 50 minutes. Serve warm with Herb Butter (page 30).

CRACKED WHEAT BREAD

Makes 1 loaf

½ cup cracked wheat
2½ cups buttermilk
¼ cup honey
2 tablespoons molasses
½ cup rye flour
3 cups whole wheat flour
2 teaspoons baking soda

Soak the cracked wheat in the buttermilk overnight.

Preheat oven to 300°F. Oil a 9 ×5-inch loaf pan.

Add the honey and molasses to the cracked wheat-buttermilk mixture; stir well.

In a separate large bowl, combine the rye flour, whole wheat flour, and baking soda. Add to the moist ingredients; mix well.

Pour into the loaf pan. Bake 1½ hours. Serve warm with Safflower Butter (page 30).

DATE AND WHEAT GERM MUFFINS

Makes 18 muffins

1 cup whole wheat flour
1 cup wheat germ
¼ cup sesame seeds
⅓ cup nonfat dry milk
3 teaspoons baking soda
1 cup milk
2 eggs, beaten
⅔ cup honey
⅓ cup safflower oil
1 cup chopped dates

Preheat oven to 400°F. Oil enough cups in muffin tins for 18 muffins or line cups with paper baking cups.

In a large bowl, mix flour, wheat germ, sesame seeds, nonfat milk, and baking soda.

In a separate medium-size bowl, combine milk, eggs, honey, and oil. Add to flour mixture, and blend well. Add chopped dates; stir until evenly distributed.

Spoon mixture into muffin cups.

Bake until lightly browned, 20 to 25 minutes.

HERBED BISCUITS

Makes 10 to 12 biscuits

2 cups whole wheat pastry flour
⅓ cup wheat germ
2 teaspoons baking powder
½ teaspoon baking soda
½ teaspoon dried basil
½ teaspoon dried marjoram
  dash of garlic powder
6 tablespoons butter, chilled
⅔ cup buttermilk or yogurt (page 24)

Preheat oven to 450°F. In a medium-size bowl, combine flour, 1 tablespoon wheat germ, baking powder, baking soda, basil, marjoram, and garlic powder. With a fork or pastry blender, cut in butter until mixture resembles coarse crumbs. Add the buttermilk or yogurt; mix.

Turn the dough out onto a work surface covered with the remaining wheat germ. Roll the dough in the wheat germ to a ¾-inch thickness. With a biscuit cutter or glass, cut into 10 to 12 biscuits.

Place on a baking sheet and bake until lightly browned, about 12 minutes. Serve warm with Safflower Butter (page 30).

HONEY-PUMPKIN MUFFINS

Makes 15 muffins

1½ cups whole wheat flour
1 tablespoon baking powder
½ teaspoon ground cinnamon
¼ teaspoon ground nutmeg
½ cup honey
1 egg
⅔ cup mashed pumpkin
⅓ cup milk
½ cup safflower oil
½ cup raisins
½ cup pecans or sunflower seeds

Preheat oven to 400°F. Oil enough cups in muffin tins for 15 muffins or line cups with paper baking cups.

In a large bowl, combine the flour, baking powder, cinnamon, and nutmeg.

In a medium-size bowl, beat the honey, egg, pumpkin, milk, and oil. Add to the dry ingredients and stir until flour is moistened.

Stir in the raisins, and pecans or sunflower seeds.

Pour batter into muffin cups to two-thirds full. Bake for 20 minutes. Serve warm or cool with Lemon-Honey Butter (page 29).

MAPLE-ORANGE BRAN MUFFINS

Makes 15 muffins

1 cup whole wheat flour
1 tablespoon baking powder
1 cup bran
½ cup wheat germ
⅓ cup nonfat dry milk
1 cup yogurt (page 24)
¼ cup orange juice
1 tablespoon grated orange rind
2 eggs, beaten
⅓ cup maple syrup
¼ cup safflower oil
½ cup raisins
½ cup chopped walnuts

Preheat oven to 400°F. Oil enough cups in muffin tins for 15 muffins or line cups with paper baking cups.

In a large bowl, mix flour, baking powder, bran, wheat germ, and nonfat dry milk.

In a medium-size bowl, combine yogurt, orange juice, orange rind, eggs, maple syrup, and oil. Add to flour mixture; stir just enough to moisten dry ingredients. Stir in raisins and walnuts.

Divide batter evenly among the muffin cups. Bake until lightly browned, 15 to 20 minutes. Serve warm with Apple Butter (page 29).

QUICK BREAD STICKS

Makes 48 bread sticks

2   cups whole wheat flour
½   cup wheat germ
½   cup cornmeal
½   cup rolled oats
⅓   cup sesame seeds
    dash of pepper
½   cup safflower oil
½   cup water
¼   cup honey

Preheat oven to 350°F. Oil 2 baking sheets.

In a large bowl, mix flour, wheat germ, cornmeal, oats, sesame seeds, and pepper.

In a small bowl, combine oil, water, and honey. Stir into the flour mixture.

On a floured board, roll the dough to a ½-inch thickness. Cut into 4 × ½-inch sticks. Place on baking sheets.

Bake until lightly browned, 20 to 25 minutes.

SPICY CARROT MUFFINS

Makes 20 muffins

1½ cups whole wheat flour
½   cup wheat germ
½   cup bran
4   tablespoons sesame seeds
1   teaspoon baking soda
1   tablespoon ground cinnamon
1   teaspoon ground nutmeg
½   teaspoon ground allspice
¼   teaspoon ground cloves
1¼ cups orange juice
⅔   cup honey
⅓   cup safflower oil
¼   cup yogurt (page 24)
3   carrots, grated
1   cup chopped pecans

Preheat oven to 350°F. Oil enough cups in muffin tins for 20 muffins or line the cups with paper baking cups.

In a large bowl, combine the flour, wheat germ, bran, sesame seeds, baking soda, cinnamon, nutmeg, allspice, and cloves.

In a medium-size bowl, mix the orange juice, honey, oil, and yogurt. Add to the flour mixture; stir until dry ingredients are moistened. Add the carrots and pecans; mix until evenly distributed.

Spoon into muffin tins. Bake 25 minutes. Serve warm with Tangerine Cream Cheese (page 33).

TOFU BREAD STICKS

½ pound firm tofu, drained
6 tablespoons butter, at room temperature
1¼ teaspoons baking powder
1 cup whole wheat flour
¼ cup sesame seeds, toasted
3 tablespoons wheat germ

Preheat oven to 375°F. Oil a baking sheet.

In a large bowl, beat with a mixer tofu, butter, and baking powder until smooth. Add the flour, sesame seeds, and wheat germ; beat until dough is smooth and elastic, about 2 minutes.

For each breadstick, place 1 heaping tablespoon dough on a work surface. Roll the dough into 5 × ½-inch sticks; place 1 inch apart on baking sheet.

Bake until lightly browned, about 35 minutes. Serve warm or at room temperature.

DESSERTS

CAROB CHIP COOKIES

1 cup butter, at room temperature
1¼ cups honey
3 eggs, beaten
1 teaspoon vanilla extract
¼ cup nonfat dry milk
2 tablespoons water
2½ cups whole wheat flour
½ cup wheat germ
1 teaspoon baking soda
2 cups carob chips
1 cup sunflower seeds
½ cup chopped walnuts

Preheat oven to 375°F. Oil baking sheets.

In a large bowl, cream the butter; add honey, eggs, vanilla, nonfat dry milk, and water; beat until fluffy.

In a separate large bowl, stir together the flour, wheat germ, and baking soda. Add to the creamed mixture and blend well.

Add the carob chips, sunflower seeds, and walnuts; mix until evenly distributed.

Drop by teaspoonfuls onto baking sheets; bake until lightly browned, 10 to 12 minutes.

These cookies freeze very nicely.

CAROB-HONEY BROWNIES WITH
CAROB-PEANUT BUTTER FROSTING

Makes 9 brownies

½ cup butter
½ cup honey
2 eggs
1 teaspoon vanilla extract
⅔ cup whole wheat flour
½ cup carob powder
¼ cup wheat germ
1 teaspoon baking powder
⅓ cup yogurt (page 24)
1 cup chopped nuts (walnuts,
    pecans, or peanuts)
    Carob-Peanut Butter Frosting (see
    following recipe)

Preheat oven to 350°F. Oil a 9×9-inch baking pan.

In a large bowl, cream the butter; add the honey. Beat in the eggs, one at a time. Beat in the vanilla.

In a separate medium-size bowl, combine the whole wheat flour, carob powder, wheat germ, and baking powder. Add to the creamed mixture. Stir in the yogurt; then add the nuts.

Pour into the baking pan. Bake until brownies spring back when lightly touched in the center with a finger-tip, about 30 minutes. Cool on a wire rack. Frost with Carob-Peanut Butter Frosting.

Carob-Peanut Butter Frosting

Yields about 1¼ cups

½ cup carob powder
½ cup water
½ cup chunky peanut butter
¼ cup honey

In a small saucepan, mix the carob powder and water; stir until smooth. Bring to a boil over low heat, stirring constantly. Cook about 3 minutes.

Remove pan from heat and stir in peanut butter and honey. Mix well. Spread over Carob-Honey Brownies.

If the frosting cools before being spread on the brownies, soften it to spreading consistency by stirring in a few drops of warm water.

CAROB-DIPPED STRAWBERRIES

Makes 1 quart

1 cup carob chips
½ cup butter
2 pints fresh strawberries,
    stems intact

In the top of a double boiler, melt the carob chips and butter.

Holding the strawberries by their stems, dip each berry far enough into the carob-butter mixture to cover about ¾ of the berry. Place the berries, stems up, on wire racks to allow coating to set. Refrigerate.

Serve the strawberries attractively arranged on a platter with other fresh chilled fruits: pineapple wedges, grapes, orange sections, apple wedges (skins intact), peach slices, kiwi slices.

Cherries make an excellent substitute for strawberries in this recipe. Use frozen cherries with stems for easiest dipping.

COCONUT-HONEY DATE BARS

Makes 10 to 15 bars

1 cup whole wheat pastry flour
½ cup wheat germ
1 teaspoon baking powder
3 eggs, beaten
¾ cup honey, warmed
½ teaspoon vanilla extract
1 cup chopped walnuts
1 cup chopped dates
½ cup shredded unsweetened
    coconut

Preheat oven to 350°F. Oil a 9 × 9-inch pan.

In a large bowl, stir together the flour, wheat germ, and baking powder.

In a separate medium-size bowl, mix the eggs, honey, and vanilla. Add to the flour mixture, stirring well. Stir in the walnuts, dates, and coconut until evenly distributed.

Spread the batter in the prepared pan and bake for 35 to 40 minutes. Cool; cut into bars.

FRESH PEACH CUSTARD PIE WITH OATMEAL-WHEAT GERM CRUST

Makes 1 pie

1 Oatmeal-Wheat Germ Crust (see following recipe)
3 medium-size peaches, peeled and sliced (about 2 cups)
1 cup yogurt (page 24)
½ cup orange juice
3 eggs, beaten
⅓ cup whole wheat flour
⅓ cup honey
1 teaspoon vanilla extract
½ teaspoon ground cinnamon
½ teaspoon ground nutmeg

Prepare Oatmeal-Wheat Germ Crust; set aside. Keep oven heated to 375°F.

Place the sliced peaches in an even layer over the crust. Combine the remaining ingredients; pour over the peaches.

Bake until filling is light brown; and a knife inserted in the center comes out clean, 45 to 50 minutes. Filling will remain moist and custard-like.

This pie is best when made the same day it is to be served.

Oatmeal-Wheat Germ Crust

Makes 1 piecrust

¾ cup oatmeal
½ cup wheat germ
4 tablespoons whole wheat flour
¼ cup finely chopped walnuts
½ teaspoon ground cinnamon
⅓ cup honey
¼ cup butter
1 teaspoon vanilla extract

Preheat oven to 375°F. Lightly oil a 9-inch pie plate.

Combine the oatmeal, wheat germ, flour, nuts, and cinnamon.

Melt the butter with the honey; add the vanilla. Stir into the oatmeal mixture, blending well. Press into the pie plate. Bake until lightly browned, 8 to 12 minutes.

FRUIT PLATTER PIE WITH WHOLE WHEAT COOKIE CRUST

Makes 1 pie

1 Whole Wheat Cookie Crust (see
   following recipe)
¼ cup honey
3 tablespoons cornstarch
1¼ cups apple juice
1 teaspoon grated lemon rind
2 tablespoons lemon juice
6 cups chopped assorted fruits
   (apples, bananas, blueberries,
   seedless green grapes, kiwi,
   nectarines, oranges,
   raspberries, or strawberries)

Prepare Whole Wheat Cookie Crust; set aside.

To make the glaze: Mix the honey and cornstarch in a medium-size saucepan; slowly stir in the apple juice; mix until smooth. Stirring constantly, warm the glaze over medium heat until it comes to a boil. Continue stirring and allow the glaze to boil until it becomes clear, about 1 minute. Remove from the heat; stir in the lemon rind and lemon juice. Cool to room temperature.

In a large bowl, gently toss the assorted fruits. Pour in the glaze; toss lightly.

Pour the fruit mixture into the Whole Wheat Cookie Crust. Chill 4 hours before serving.

Whole Wheat Cookie Crust

Makes 1 piecrust

¼ cup butter, at room temperature
2 tablespoons honey
1 egg yolk, lightly beaten
½ cup whole wheat flour
½ cup wheat germ
¼ cup chopped walnuts
¼ cup shredded unsweetened
   coconut
½ teaspoon ground cinnamon
¼ teaspoon ground nutmeg

Preheat oven to 400°F.

In a medium-size bowl, cream the butter; add the honey and beat in the egg yolk.

In a separate medium-size bowl, mix the flour, wheat germ, walnuts, coconut, cinnamon, and nutmeg. Add to the creamed mixture; stir until well blended.

Press mixture into a 9-inch pie plate. Bake until lightly browned, about 10 minutes. Cool.

This crust is easily made in a food processor. To prepare: Blend together butter, honey, and egg. Add the remaining ingredients and process until the mixture forms a ball.

HONEY RICE PUDDING

6 to 8 servings

¾ cup milk
2 eggs, beaten
3 tablespoons honey
1 teaspoon vanilla extract
1½ cups cooked brown rice
½ cup wheat germ
½ cup raisins or chopped dried
     apricots

Preheat oven to 350°F. Oil a 1½-quart baking dish that has a cover.

In a large bowl, mix the milk, eggs, honey, and vanilla. Add the rice, wheat germ, and raisins or apricots; mix again. Pour into the baking dish; bake until set, 45 to 50 minutes.

Serve hot or chilled, and garnish with Apricot-Orange Sauce (page 53), if desired.

KIWI SHERBET

Yields about 3 cups

4 medium-size kiwis, peeled and
     diced
1 cup orange juice
2 tablespoons lemon juice
¼ cup honey
2 egg whites

Place the kiwi, orange juice, lemon juice, and honey in a blender or food processor; process until smooth. Pour into a shallow tray and freeze until almost solid.

Remove from freezer and turn into a medium-size bowl. Beat with a mixer until smooth and slushy.

In a small bowl, beat the egg whites until soft peaks form; fold into the kiwi mixture. Pour into a plastic container, cover, and freeze until firm.

NUT-CRUSTED RICOTTA CHEESECAKE WITH LEMON GLAZE

Makes 1 cheesecake

1¼ cups whole wheat flour
¼ cup wheat germ
½ cup finely chopped pecans
¼ cup shredded fresh coconut
½ cup butter
2 tablespoons honey
1½ cups ricotta cheese (12 ounces)
1½ cups kefir cheese or cream cheese (12 ounces)
1 cup yogurt (page 24)
⅔ cup honey
8 eggs
2 teaspoons vanilla extract
1½ cups Lemon Glaze (see following recipe), Honey-Raspberry Sauce (page 98), or sliced fresh fruit

Preheat oven to 375°F.

In a large bowl, mix the flour, wheat germ, pecans, and coconut.

Melt the butter with the honey; gradually pour into the dry ingredients, stirring with a fork as you pour. Press onto the bottom and sides (to within ½-inch of the top) of a 9-inch springform pan. Bake for 10 minutes. Remove from oven and set aside.

Reduce oven temperature to 325°F.

In a food processor or blender, process the cheeses, yogurt, honey, eggs, and vanilla until smooth. Ladle into partially baked crust. Bake until lightly browned on top and a toothpick inserted in the center comes out clean, 70 to 80 minutes.

Chill 5 to 6 hours. Remove from springform pan and place on a serving platter. Top with Lemon Glaze, Honey Raspberry Sauce, or sliced fresh fruit. To serve, slice into thin wedges.

Lemon Glaze

Yields about 1½ cups

1 cup water
1½ tablespoons cornstarch
5 tablespoons honey
⅓ cup lemon juice
2 teaspoons grated lemon rind

In a small saucepan, gradually add water to cornstarch, stirring until smooth. Place over low heat and cook until cornstarch is dissolved. Add remaining ingredients and bring to a boil over medium heat, stirring constantly until smooth and clear. Cool. Spread on Nut-Crusted Ricotta Cheesecake.

PAPAYA SHERBET

Yields about 3 cups

1 large papaya, peeled and diced
1 cup orange juice
¼ cup honey
2 egg whites

Place the papaya, orange juice, and honey in a blender or food processor; process until smooth. Pour into a shallow tray and freeze until almost solid.

Remove from the freezer and turn into medium-size mixing bowl. Beat with a mixer until smooth and slushy.

In a separate small bowl, beat the egg whites until soft peaks form; fold into papaya mixture. Pour into a plastic container, cover, and freeze until firm.

PEACH MELBA WITH HONEY-RASPBERRY SAUCE

6 servings

3 medium-size peaches, peeled and halved
3 cups yogurt (page 24)
Honey-Raspberry Sauce (see following recipe)

Place peach halves in dessert dishes, parfait glasses, or large goblets. Top each with ½ cup yogurt. Spoon about ¼ cup Honey-Raspberry Sauce over each serving. Serve immediately.

Honey-Raspberry Sauce

Yields 1 cup

2 cups fresh or frozen raspberries
3 tablespoons honey
2 teaspoons cornstarch
¼ cup water

In a small saucepan, combine berries and honey. Cook over low heat, stirring constantly, until just below boiling. Remove from heat.

In a small bowl, mix cornstarch and water until smooth; add to the berry-honey mixture. Stirring constantly, cook over low heat until thick and smooth, 5 to 7 minutes.

Strain sauce through a coarse sieve; cool. Place in a container, cover, and store in the refrigerator.

This sauce makes a delicious topping for yogurt, cheesecake, pancakes, and dessert crepes.

SAUTÉED APPLE SLICES AND ORANGE-PEACH SAUCE

6 servings

10 large dried peaches
⅓ cup orange juice
3 tablespoons butter
½ cup sliced almonds
3 large baking apples, peeled, and cut into ⅜-inch slices
1 tablespoon honey
1 teaspoon vanilla extract

To make the Orange-Peach Sauce: Place dried peaches in a large bowl and cover with hot water. Set aside to soften, 10 to 15 minutes; drain. Puree the peaches in a food processor or blender. Add the orange juice and blend until smooth. Transfer to a container, cover, and chill until serving time.

Melt 1 tablespoon butter in a large skillet over low heat. Add almonds and stir over medium heat until lightly browned. Remove from pan and set aside.

Melt the remaining butter in the skillet over low heat. Add apple slices, honey, and vanilla. Cook over high heat, tossing with a spatula until apples are warmed through and tender but still crisp.

To serve: Arrange about 6 apple slices on each dessert plate; top with warmed Orange-Peach Sauce; sprinkle with sliced almonds. Serve while apples are still warm.

STRAWBERRY-RHUBARB PIE WITH WHOLE WHEAT PASTRY

Makes 1 pie

Whole Wheat Pastry (see
  following recipe)
1 cup honey
⅓ cup whole wheat flour
½ teaspoon grated orange rind
2 cups chopped rhubarb
3 cups sliced fresh strawberries
2 tablespoons butter

Prepare Whole Wheat Pastry. Set aside. Preheat oven to 350°F.

In a large bowl, mix the honey, flour, and orange rind. Add rhubarb and strawberries; stir until evenly distributed. Pour into bottom crust. Dot with the butter. Cover with top crust. Slit, seal, and flute the edges. Cover the edges with a 2 or 3-inch strip of foil.

Bake for 40 to 50 minutes; remove foil the last 15 minutes of baking.

For a Honey-Rhubarb Pie, omit the strawberries and use 5 cups of chopped rhubarb.

Whole Wheat Pastry

Makes 2 crusts

2 cups whole wheat pastry flour
¾ cup unsalted butter
¼ cup ground pecans or walnuts
1 teaspoon cider vinegar
1 egg, beaten
2 to 3 tablespoons ice water

In a medium-size bowl, cut the butter into the flour. Add the pecans or walnuts, vinegar, egg, and 2 tablespoons of the water. Mix with a fork, or process in a food processor until the mixture forms a ball. Add the remaining tablespoon water only if necessary to make the dough moist enough to form a ball.

Chill the ball of dough for 1 hour and slice it in half. On a work surface, roll out each half between two sheets of waxed paper.

VANILLA-POACHED PEARS WITH HONEY-VANILLA CUSTARD

6 pears
3 tablespoons vanilla extract
3 tablespoons honey
3 cups Honey-Vanilla Custard (see
    following recipe)

Peel the pears; cut in half and place in a Dutch oven. Cover with water.

Combine the vanilla and honey; add to the poaching water. Bring to a boil; reduce heat, cover, and simmer until the pears are just tender but not soft, about 15 minutes. Remove the pears from the water, place in a dish, and refrigerate.

To serve, place pears in dessert bowls; spoon about ½ cup of Honey-Vanilla Custard over each portion.

Honey-Vanilla Custard

Yields 3 cups

3 cups milk
3 tablespoons cornstarch
⅓ cup honey
3 egg yolks, lightly beaten
1½ teaspoons vanilla extract
1 tablespoon butter

In a medium-size saucepan, combine milk, cornstarch, and honey; mix well. Cook over low heat, stirring constantly, until mixture thickens. Remove from heat.

In a small bowl, stir about ¼ cup of the warm honey-milk mixture into the egg yolks; pour into the saucepan. Place the mixture over low heat and cook, stirring constantly, until the custard is thick, smooth, and creamy, about 15 minutes. Add the vanilla and stir; add the butter and stir until melted.

Cover and chill.

WALNUT TORTE

4 eggs, separated
½ cup honey
  grated rind of 1 lemon
3 cups ground walnuts

Preheat oven to 375°F. Oil and dust with flour a deep 9-inch baking pan or a springform pan.

In a large bowl, beat the egg yolks, add the honey, and beat again until light-colored and fluffy. Stir in the lemon rind.

In a separate bowl, beat the egg whites until they will form stiff peaks; fold about ½ cup of the whites into the yolk mixture. Beat the walnuts into the yolks until throughly blended. Fold in the remaining whites.

Pour the batter into the prepared pan. Bake until the top is firm and golden brown, but the interior is still moist, 20 to 30 minutes. Allow the torte to cool on a wire rack before removing it from the pan.

WHITE GRAPE MOUSSE

3 tablespoons unflavored gelatin
3 cups white grape juice
1 pound seedless white grapes
1 teaspoon vanilla extract
1 cup heavy cream, whipped
2 tablespoons honey
  grape clusters

Chill a 1½-quart soufflé dish.

In a small saucepan, combine the gelatin with 1 cup of the grape juice; let stand to soften, 5 minutes. Place over low heat, stirring constantly, until gelatin dissolves. Cool to room temperature. Stir in the remaining grape juice. Pour a ½-inch layer into the bottom of a soufflé dish. Chill until the mixture reaches the consistency of egg whites.

Cut into halves ¾ of the loose grapes; set aside and arrange the remainder in a decorative pattern on top of the nearly set gelatin. Spoon on another thin layer of gelatin mixture and chill again to set the design.

Pour the remaining gelatin mixture into a separate bowl and chill until the mixture reaches the consistency of egg whites. Into this mixture stir the vanilla and halved grapes.

Fold the honey into the whipped cream, then fold into the gelatin mixture in the bowl. Spoon into the soufflé dish. Cover and chill until the mousse is completely set, 5 to 6 hours.

Unmold to serve. Garnish with small clusters of grapes at the base of the mold.

The mousse may also be frozen. Allow to soften partially before serving.

Family Dinners

Mealtime is a precious part of family life. I do my best to make our time together festive and the food interesting. Some of the menus in this section are for special family occasions; others are perfect for everyday fare. When organizing the menus, I often find it difficult to separate family dishes from those intended for guests. That's because I truly believe my family is as important as any special company I invite to my home. Anything I offer my family I'd proudly serve to guests.

To help make family dinners memorable, I like to use centerpieces, candles, and serving platters. Adding these amenities takes only a few minutes, and I know the family appreciates the little bit of extra effort. Then I present such tempting dishes as Nutburgers, Quick Cashew Creole, and Creamy Tomato-Vegetable Soup, to name but a few of the recipes in this section.

MENUS

FAMILY DINNERS

꒰ Herbed Cheese-Vegetable Melange
Quick Caesar Salad
Maple-Sauced Oranges

꒰ Nutburgers
Orange-Tahini Green Beans
Curried Tomato-Rice Salad
Honey-Pumpkin Mousse

꒰ Kidney Bean-Corn Pie
Avocado-Sprout Salad
Pineapple Frost

꒰ Pureed Vegetable Soup with Walnut-Cheese Nuggets
Oriental Pea Pod-Tomato Salad
Apple-Raisin Bran Muffins
Frozen Apricot-Orange Mousse

꒰ Cumin Cucumber Salad
Whole Wheat-Orange Toast
Avocado Omelets
Banana Frozen Yogurt

꒰ Quick Cashew Creole
Veggie Rice
Cucumber-Carrot Salad
Apricot Whip

꒰ Cashew Chili
Mixed Grain-Honey Corn Bread
Garden Salad with Creamy Garlic Dressing
Apple Crisp

Ɏ Peppers Stuffed with Tofu and Rice
Bean Sprout-Apple Salad
Molasses-Rye Muffins
Carob-Pineapple Cream

Ɏ Creamy Tomato-Vegetable Soup
Cheesy Broccoli Shortcake over Flaky Brown Rice Biscuits
Spinach-Apple Salad
Honey-Carrot Cake with Kefir Cheese Frosting

Ɏ Caraway-Dill-Potato Soup
Sunshine Carrot Salad
Rye Biscuits
Maple-Yogurt Gingerbread with Honey-Lemon Sauce

Ɏ Carrot-Nut Loaf with Lemony Spinach Sauce
Mushroom Rice
Fruity Sprout Salad
Carob Creme Patisserie

Ɏ Mushroom-Crusted Cheese Pie
Tomatoes Provençal
Spinach-Avocado Salad with Lemon-Mustard Vinaigrette
Baked Bananas with Raisin-Walnut Sauce

Ɏ Eggplant-Celery Pizza
Endive and Apple Salad with Celery Seed Dressing
Fresh Fruit Fondue

Ɏ Lentil Loaf with Cashew Gravy
Maple Squash
Carrot-Sprout Slaw
Baked Apples in Orange Sauce

Ɏ Zucchini Stuffed with Lentils and Tomatoes
Walnut-Wild Rice Pilaf
Vegetable Salad with Creamy Herb Dressing
Spicy Apple Cake with Orange-Raisin Sauce

MAIN COURSES

AVOCADO OMELETS

2 **medium-size avocados**
3 **tablespoons yogurt (page 24) or Mayonnaise (page 31)**
2 **tablespoons lemon juice**
2 **tablespoons minced onion**
¼ **teaspoon pepper**
   dash of hot pepper sauce
8 **eggs**
4 **tablespoons cold water**
4 **tablespoons butter**
1 **tomato, at room temperature, sliced**
2 **tablespoons chopped fresh parsley**
½ **cup alfalfa sprouts**
1 **orange, cut into quarters**
1 **cup yogurt (page 24) or sour cream**
   Tomato Hot Sauce (page 34)

Cut avocados in half, and chop. Set aside the pit. Place avocado in a small bowl and mash with a fork; add the yogurt or mayonnaise, lemon juice, onion, pepper, and hot pepper sauce. Mix thoroughly. For a smoother texture, process in a food processor or blender. Set aside and place the reserved avocado pit in this mixture to help prevent darkening!

For each omelet, beat 2 eggs with 1 tablespoon cold water. In an 8-inch omelet pan or skillet, melt 1 tablespoon butter over medium heat. Pour in the egg mixture; stir with a fork, tilting the pan occasionally so uncooked eggs can flow to the bottom. While the top still looks moist and creamy, spread about ⅓ cup of the avocado mixture down the center of the omelet. Fold the two edges of the omelet over, reduce heat to low, cover, and allow to heat for a minute. Turn omelet onto a warmed plate and place in a 200°F oven to keep warm while remaining servings are being prepared.

Garnish each omelet with a tomato slice, sprouts, and parsley. Place an orange wedge to the side.

Serve with the yogurt or sour cream, and Tomato Hot Sauce.

CARROT-NUT LOAF WITH LEMONY SPINACH SAUCE

6 servings

1 tablespoon safflower oil
1 medium-size onion, chopped
1 clove garlic, minced
2 cups whole grain bread crumbs
4 medium-size carrots, grated
1 cup ground walnuts
1 egg, beaten
2 tablespoons milk
1 tablespoon fresh parsley
½ teaspoon pepper
¼ teaspoon ground nutmeg
   Lemony Spinach Sauce (see following recipe)

Preheat oven to 350°F. Oil an 8½ × 4½-inch loaf pan.

In a medium-size saucepan, heat the oil. Sauté the onion and garlic until lightly browned. Stir in the remaining ingredients, except the Lemony Spinach Sauce.

Press the mixture into the loaf pan. Bake for 30 minutes.

Serve with Lemony Spinach Sauce.

Leftover Carrot-Nut Loaf is delicious when sliced and eaten cold, or dipped in egg and fried in oil.

Lemony Spinach Sauce

6 servings

1½ pounds spinach
3 tablespoons butter
3 tablespoons whole wheat flour
2 teaspoons grated lemon rind
2 tablespoons lemon juice
   freshly ground pepper, to taste
1½ cups yogurt (page 24)

Rinse spinach well. In a large saucepan, cook spinach, covered, without water except for the drops that cling to the leaves. Reduce heat when steam forms and cook 2 to 3 minutes. Do not drain; puree with liquid in a food processor or blender.

Melt the butter; stir in the flour. Cook, stirring constantly, about 3 minutes. Add spinach puree and cook about 5 minutes, stirring constantly. Add the lemon rind, lemon juice, and pepper. Just before serving whisk in the yogurt; heat gently but do not allow the mixture to boil.

CASHEW CHILI

8 servings

3 tablespoons butter
1 medium-size onion, chopped
1 green pepper, chopped
2 stalks celery, chopped
2 cups cooked kidney beans, drained
1½ cups (2 8-ounce cans) tomato sauce
2 cups cooked corn
2 cups (18-ounce can) whole tomatoes
2 to 3 teaspoons chili powder
3 drops hot pepper sauce
1 teaspoon ground cumin
2 cloves garlic, minced
1 teaspoon dried basil
1 teaspoon dried oregano
1 bay leaf
½ teaspoon pepper
1 cup raisins
1 cup whole raw cashews
Monterey Jack or cheddar cheese, grated

In a large saucepan or Dutch oven, melt the butter. Sauté the onion, green pepper, and celery until crisp-tender, about 10 minutes.

Add the beans, tomato sauce, corn, tomatoes, chili powder, pepper sauce, cumin, garlic, basil, oregano, bay leaf, and pepper. Bring to a boil; reduce heat and simmer 30 minutes to blend flavors.

Stir in the raisins and cashews; continue to simmer until the raisins are plump and the cashews are tender, about 20 minutes.

To serve, ladle into bowls and top each serving with grated cheese. Serve with additional cheese.

CHEESY BROCCOLI SHORTCAKE OVER FLAKY BROWN RICE BISCUITS

4 to 6 servings

2 cups brown rice flour
4 teaspoons baking powder
1⅓ cups milk
⅓ cup safflower oil
1 tablespoon water
2 tablespoons butter
2 tablespoons whole wheat flour
1 cup grated cheddar cheese
    (4 ounces)
¼ teaspoon ground nutmeg
¼ teaspoon pepper
4 cups coarsely chopped broccoli,
    steamed until crisp-tender
paprika

Preheat oven to 400°F.

To prepare the biscuits: Combine brown rice flour and baking powder in a medium-size bowl.

In a separate small bowl, combine ⅔ cup milk, oil, and water. Stir to mix thoroughly.

Add the milk mixture to the dry ingredients, stirring just enough to moisten all of the flour. The dough should be crumbly. With your hands, form the dough into a ball and place on a board lightly floured with brown rice flour.

Knead the dough briefly, merely folding it over a few times. With a rolling pin, roll the dough to a uniform ½-inch thickness. With a biscuit cutter or a glass 2½ inches in diameter, cut the dough into 8 or 9 circles.

Place the biscuits on an ungreased baking sheet and bake until they are light brown, about 15 minutes.

While the biscuits are baking, prepare the cheese sauce. In a small saucepan, melt the butter over low heat. Remove from heat and stir in the whole wheat flour. Cook over low heat, stirring constantly, until mixture is smooth and bubbly. Stir in the remaining milk, increase the heat to medium, and stir constantly until the mixture starts to boil. Add the cheese, nutmeg, and pepper, stirring constantly until the cheese has melted.

Add the broccoli to the cheese sauce. Stir until the broccoli is heated through.

To serve, place 1 or 2 warm biscuits in the bottom of each bowl. Pour a generous serving of the cheese sauce over the biscuits. Garnish each serving with a sprinkling of paprika.

EGGPLANT-CELERY PIZZA

2 cups whole wheat flour
1 tablespoon dry yeast
1 cup warm water (about 85°F)
2 tablespoons safflower oil
1 teaspoon honey
1 clove garlic, minced
1 cup sliced mushrooms
¼ cup chopped onion
1½ cups (15-ounce can) tomato puree
1 teaspoon chopped fresh parsley
½ teaspoon dried oregano
½ teaspoon dried basil
¼ teaspoon pepper
1 cup cubed eggplant
½ cup chopped celery
½ cup chopped green pepper
¼ cup sliced almonds
2 tablespoons olive oil
1½ cups shredded mozzarella cheese
        (6 ounces)

To make the crust: Combine the flour and yeast in a large bowl. In a cup, combine the water, 1 tablespoon of the oil, and the honey. Pour into the flour mixture and beat vigorously until well mixed. Cover the bowl with plastic wrap and set in a warm place to rise for 10 to 15 minutes.

Meanwhile, oil a 14-inch pizza pan and preheat oven to 425°F.

Punch down the dough and place in the prepared pan. Press with fingers to cover the bottom of the pan and pinch up the sides to the rim. Bake for 8 minutes.

To make the sauce: Heat the remaining oil in a medium-size saucepan; sauté the garlic, mushrooms, and onion until tender. Stir in the tomato puree, parsley, oregano, basil, and pepper. Bring mixture to a boil; reduce heat and simmer, uncovered, for 15 to 20 minutes to reduce the sauce slightly and to combine flavors.

Spread the sauce evenly over the partially baked crust. Arrange the eggplant, celery, green pepper, and almonds evenly over the top. Sprinkle on the olive oil; top with the cheese.

Bake until the crust is browned and the cheese is melted.

KIDNEY BEAN-CORN PIE

1 cup cornmeal
6 tablespoons safflower oil
½ cup Vegetable Stock (page 35)
1 medium-size onion, chopped
1 stalk celery, chopped
½ medium-size green pepper,
    chopped
1 clove garlic, minced
2 cups cooked kidney beans,
    drained
1 cup cooked corn, drained
1 cup tomato sauce
⅓ cup roasted unsalted peanuts
2 teaspoons chili powder
½ teaspoon ground cumin
½ teaspoon dried oregano
½ teaspoon pepper
2 drops hot pepper sauce
½ cup grated cheddar cheese
    (2 ounces)
½ cup grated Monterey Jack cheese
    (2 ounces)

Preheat oven to 350°F. Oil an 8-inch deep-dish quiche pan or a 9-inch pie plate.

In a small bowl, combine cornmeal, 4 tablespoons oil, and ¼ cup vegetable stock. Mix thoroughly with a fork. Press into the prepared pan; set aside.

Heat 2 tablespoons oil in a large skillet. Add onion, celery, green pepper, and garlic. Cook until onion is softened but not browned. Stir in remaining vegetable stock and all other ingredients except the cheeses.

In a small bowl, toss together the two cheeses. Spread about ⅓ of the cheese mixture on the cornmeal crust; pour in the bean mixture and spread evenly. Bake about 30 minutes.

Remove from the oven and cover with the remaining cheese. Return the pan to the oven until the cheese has melted, about 10 minutes.

Let the pie set for 5 to 10 minutes before cutting into wedges for serving.

The crust and the filling can be made in advance. Press the crust into the pan, cover, and refrigerate. Keep the filling in a covered container. Bring each to room temperature, fill the crust, and bake the pie just before serving time.

LENTIL LOAF WITH CASHEW GRAVY

6 to 8 servings

1½ cups cooked lentils
1½ cups cooked brown rice
½ cup peas, cooked
1 egg, beaten
½ cup whole grain bread crumbs
½ cup finely ground nuts (raw cashews, almonds, or pecans)
¼ cup rolled oats
¼ cup finely ground sunflower seeds
¼ cup chopped onion
4 tablespoons safflower oil
2 tablespoons tomato paste
½ teaspoon dried sage
½ teaspoon celery seed
1 clove garlic, minced
2 tablespoons sesame seeds
Cashew Gravy (see following recipe)
⅓ cup chopped fresh parsley

Preheat oven to 350°F. Oil a 9 × 5-inch loaf pan.

In a large bowl, combine all ingredients except sesame seeds, gravy, and parsley. Stir until well blended.

Spoon the mixture into the loaf pan. Sprinkle with sesame seeds.

Bake until loaf is firm and top is lightly browned, about 45 minutes.

Serve topped with Cashew Gravy and garnished with chopped parsley

Leftover Lentil Loaf is delicious in cold or hot sandwiches.

Cashew Gravy

Yields about 2¼ cups

2 cups water
¼ cup raw cashews
1 tablespoon soy sauce
1 tablespoon sesame oil

In a food processor or blender, combine the water, cashews, soy sauce, and sesame oil. Process until the mixture is very smooth.

Transfer the mixture to a medium-size saucepan. Cook over medium heat, stirring constantly, until the mixture thickens, about 5 minutes.

Serve warm over Lentil Loaf.

PEPPERS STUFFED WITH TOFU AND RICE

Makes 6 peppers

3 tablespoons safflower or olive oil
1 medium-size onion, chopped
2 cloves garlic, minced
1 stalk celery, chopped
1 medium-size carrot, grated
⅓ cup chopped pecans
1 pound drained firm tofu, mashed
1⅔ cups (15-ounce can) tomato sauce
1½ cups cooked brown rice
½ cup grated cheddar cheese
    (2 ounces)
1 tablespoon soy sauce
¼ teaspoon dried basil
¼ teaspoon dried oregano
¼ teaspoon pepper
2 eggs, beaten
6 large green peppers
¼ cup wheat germ
¼ cup grated Parmesan cheese
    (1 ounce)
¾ to 1 cup boiling water

In a large skillet, heat 2 tablespoons oil. Stir in the onion, garlic, celery, and carrot; sauté until vegetables are tender, about 5 minutes. Remove pan from the heat and stir in the pecans, tofu, tomato sauce, brown rice, cheddar cheese, soy sauce, basil, oregano, and pepper. When mixture is slightly cooled, stir in the eggs.

Preheat oven to 350°F.

Remove tops and centers from peppers; spoon the tofu-rice mixture into the peppers. Place the peppers upright in a baking dish.

In a small bowl, combine the wheat germ, Parmesan cheese, and 1 tablespoon oil; sprinkle this mixture over the stuffed peppers.

Pour boiling water around the peppers to ¼ up the sides of the baking dish. Bake until the peppers are tender when pierced with a fork, about 30 minutes. Check occasionally during the baking period and add more water if necessary.

If the peppers will not accommodate all of the filling, bake extra filling in an oiled casserole dish.

HERBED CHEESE-VEGETABLE MELANGE

6 servings

8 tablespoons butter
2 tablespoons whole wheat flour
1 cup milk
1 cup grated cheddar or colby
      cheese (4 ounces)
1 teaspoon dried basil
      freshly ground pepper, to taste
6 baked potatoes, kept hot
8 cups assorted sliced vegetables,
      (broccoli, cauliflower, zucchini,
      carrots, celery, mushrooms)
2 tablespoons chopped fresh parsley
1 large tomato, cut into ½-inch
      cubes
⅓ cup sliced almonds

To make Herbed Cheese: In a small saucepan, melt 2 tablespoons butter over low heat. Remove pan from the heat and stir in the flour. Cook over low heat, stirring until the mixture is smooth and bubbly. Stir in the milk; increase the heat to medium, bring to a boil, and add the cheese, basil, and pepper, stirring constantly until the cheese has melted.

To assemble the Vegetable Melange: Split the potatoes into halves. In each of 6 small bowls, place a halved potato, and spread 1 tablespoon butter on each.

In a large bowl, gently toss vegetables. Stir in the parsley and tomato. Spoon about 1½ cups of the vegetable mixture onto each potato.

Top each serving with the warm Herbed Cheese, and garnish with about 1 tablespoon sliced almonds. Serve immediately.

MUSHROOM-CRUSTED CHEESE PIE

6 servings

3 tablespoons butter
1 tablespoon lemon juice
½ pound fresh mushrooms, minced
½ cup finely crushed unsalted whole
      wheat crackers
2 tablespoons poppy seeds
3 scallions, chopped
1 cup cottage cheese
3 eggs
2 cups shredded Monterey Jack or
      Swiss cheese (8 ounces)
½ teaspoon dried basil
¼ teaspoon dried marjoram
      dash of cayenne pepper
      dash of paprika

Preheat oven to 350°F.
Oil a 9-inch pie plate.
In a skillet, melt 2 tablespoons of the butter over medium heat. Add the lemon juice and mushrooms; cook until the mushrooms are limp. Stir in the cracker crumbs and poppy seeds. Turn this mixture into the prepared pie plate; press into bottom and sides of pan. Bake for 15 minutes.

In the same skillet, melt the remaining butter over medium heat. Add the scallions and cook until limp; set aside.

In a food processor or blender, process the cottage cheese and eggs until smooth. Stir in the scallions, cheese, basil, marjoram, and cayenne pepper. Pour into the partially baked crust; sprinkle with paprika.

Bake for 25 minutes. Let stand 10 to 15 minutes before serving.

NUTBURGERS

4 eggs, beaten
½ cup chopped walnuts
¼ cup chopped almonds
¼ cup sunflower seeds
¼ cup wheat germ
1 cup shredded cheddar cheese
    (4 ounces)
1 medium-size onion, chopped
½ cup finely grated carrot
¼ cup finely chopped celery
2 tablespoons sesame seeds
1 tablespoon chopped fresh parsley
2 teaspoons soy sauce
2 cloves garlic, minced
½ teaspoon dried thyme leaves
¼ cup milk
¼ cup whole wheat bread crumbs or
    whole wheat cracker crumbs
3 tablespoons safflower oil

In a medium-size bowl, combine all ingredients except oil. Blend well. Form mixture into 6 to 8 patties, ½ inch thick.

In a large skillet, heat the oil. Cook patties on both sides until browned. Drain on absorbent paper before serving.

If desired, a slice of cheese may be melted on top of each pattie before serving.

QUICK CASHEW CREOLE

6 servings

¼ cup butter
½ pound mushrooms, sliced
1 large onion, chopped
3 stalks celery, diced
1 clove garlic, minced
2 tablespoons whole wheat flour
1 teaspoon honey
1 teaspoon paprika
1 teaspoon chili powder
4 drops hot pepper sauce
    dash of cayenne pepper
1 small bay leaf
½ green pepper, diced
1 cup raw whole cashews
1 pound drained firm tofu, cut into
    1-inch cubes (optional)
1 15-ounce can tomatoes
    parsley

In a large skillet, melt the butter. Add the mushrooms, onion, celery, and garlic. Cook slowly over low heat until tender but not browned.

Add the flour, honey, paprika, chili powder, pepper sauce and cayenne; stir until well blended. Add the bay leaf, green pepper, cashews, and tofu cubes. Cut tomatoes into quarters, and add. Cook over low heat for 20 minutes, stirring occasionally. Remove bay leaf.

To serve, spread a layer of Veggie Rice in a deep serving platter; top with Quick Cashew Creole. Garnish with parsley.

ZUCCHINI STUFFED WITH LENTILS AND TOMATOES

4 to 6 servings

⅔ cup dried lentils
2 cups water
4 carrots, finely chopped
2 stalks celery, finely chopped
1 medium-size onion, finely chopped
½ green pepper, finely chopped
1 bay leaf
4 to 6 medium-size zucchinis (one per serving)
 freshly ground pepper, to taste
¾ cup (6-ounce can) tomato paste
½ cup wheat germ or whole wheat bread crumbs
¼ cup finely chopped walnuts
2 tablespoons chopped fresh parsley
2 cloves garlic, minced
1½ teaspoon dillweed
½ teaspoon dried marjoram
½ teaspoon dried tarragon
¼ teaspoon dried thyme leaves
⅓ cup grated Parmesan cheese

In a large saucepan, place lentils, water, carrots, celery, onion, green pepper, and bay leaf. Bring to a boil, reduce heat, and simmer gently until lentils are tender and nearly all liquid has been absorbed, 30 to 40 minutes.

Meanwhile, parboil zucchinis in boiling water until just tender, about 15 minutes. Drain and cool slightly.

Preheat oven to 350°F. Oil an 8 × 10-inch baking pan.

Slice each zucchini in half lengthwise. Scoop the zucchinis out and place the insides in a colander to drain. Arrange the zucchini shells in the baking pan and sprinkle with freshly ground pepper.

When the lentils are cooked, remove the bay leaf. Stir in the drained zucchini centers. Then add the tomato paste, ¼ cup wheat germ or bread crumbs, walnuts, parsley, garlic, dillweed, marjoram, tarragon, thyme, and additional pepper.

Spoon about ¼ cup of the lentil mixture into each zucchini half. Combine Parmesan cheese and remaining wheat germ or bread crumbs; sprinkle over the stuffing.

Bake for 25 to 30 minutes.

Spoon any extra stuffing into an oiled ovenproof casserole and bake along with the stuffed zucchini.

SALADS

AVOCADO-SPROUT SALAD

4 to 6 servings

1 avocado, cut into ½-inch cubes
¼ cup lemon juice
1 cup mung bean sprouts
1 cup shredded lettuce or spinach
1 scallion, chopped
½ red pepper, chopped
¼ cup safflower oil
1 teaspoon honey
  pinch of dry mustard
  freshly ground pepper

In a small bowl, toss the avocado with the lemon juice. Drain, reserving lemon juice for the dressing.

In a medium-size salad bowl, combine avocado, sprouts, lettuce or spinach, scallion, and red pepper.

In a separate small bowl, mix the remaining ingredients with the lemon juice. Pour over the avocado-sprout mixture. Serve immediately.

BEAN SPROUT-APPLE SALAD

6 servings

2 cups bean sprouts
2 apples, cubed
2 carrots, grated
¼ cup raisins
2 tablespoons lemon juice
¼ cup Mayonnaise (page 31)
1 teaspoon vanilla extract

In a large salad bowl, toss bean sprouts, apples, carrots, raisins, and 1 tablespoon lemon juice.

In a separate small bowl, combine remaining lemon juice, mayonnaise, and vanilla. Combine both mixtures just before serving.

CARROT-SPROUT SLAW

6 servings

⅓ cup Mayonnaise (page 31)
1 teaspoon vanilla extract
3 cups mixed sprouts (alfalfa, mung bean)
3 carrots, shredded
2 stalks celery, diced
¼ cup raisins
3 tablespoons minced fresh parsley
2 tablespoons minced scallions
  crisp greens

In a small bowl, combine the mayonnaise and vanilla; set aside.

In a large bowl, toss the sprouts, carrots, celery, raisins, parsley, and scallions. Add the mayonnaise mixture; toss again until the vegetables are moistened. Cover and chill.

To serve, place mounds of the Carrot-Sprout Slaw on beds of crisp greens on salad plates.

CUCUMBER-CARROT SALAD

6 servings

½ cup cider vinegar
⅓ cup water
3 tablespoons honey, warmed
1 teaspoon minced ginger root or
    ¼ teaspoon powdered ginger
1 large cucumber, thinly sliced
1 large carrot, thinly sliced
    fresh spinach or lettuce leaves

In a small bowl, combine the vinegar, water, honey, and ginger. Set aside.

In a medium-size bowl, toss the cucumber and carrot. Pour the honey-ginger marinade over the vegetables; stir gently.

Cover and refrigerate for at least 1 hour.

Serve on beds of fresh spinach or lettuce.

CUMIN CUCUMBER SALAD

4 servings

½ cup cottage cheese
½ cup yogurt (page 24)
1 tablespoon lemon juice
½ teaspoon ground cumin
¼ teaspoon pepper
1 medium-size cucumber, cut into
    ½-inch cubes
1 tomato, cut into ½-inch cubes
1 cup cubed jicama (optional)
1 scallion, chopped
    romaine lettuce leaves
¼ cup toasted sesame seeds

In a food processor or blender, process the cottage cheese, yogurt, lemon juice, cumin, and pepper. Refrigerate for at least 1 hour.

In a medium-size bowl, toss together cucumber, tomato, jicama, and scallion. Refrigerate.

To serve, place mounds of the cucumber-tomato mixture on beds of lettuce. Spoon on the dressing. Garnish with sesame seeds.

CURRIED TOMATO-RICE SALAD

6 servings

2 tablespoons safflower oil
2 tablespoons cider vinegar
1 clove garlic, minced
1 teaspoon lemon juice
1 teaspoon curry powder
2 cups cooked brown rice
1 medium-size tomato, cut into
    1-inch cubes
1 scallion, minced
2 tablespoons chopped fresh parsley
    freshly ground pepper, to taste
    romaine lettuce leaves

In a small bowl or jar, combine the oil, vinegar, garlic, lemon juice, and curry powder. Set aside.

In a medium-size bowl, toss together the rice, tomato, scallion, parsley, and pepper. Pour the curry dressing over this mixture and toss lightly with a fork. Chill until serving time.

Serve on beds of lettuce.

ENDIVE AND APPLE SALAD WITH CELERY SEED DRESSING

8 servings

8 heads Belgian endive, cut into
    1-inch slices
4 large red Delicious apples, cut
    into ½-inch cubes
¼ cup chopped pecans
⅓ cup golden raisins
¼ cup currants
    Celery Seed Dressing (see
    following recipe)
1 cup grated carrots

In a large bowl, toss endive, apples, pecans, raisins, and currants. Place in salad bowls; spoon on Celery Seed Dressing. Garnish each serving with grated carrots.

Celery Seed Dressing

Yields 1¾ cups

1 cup Mayonnaise (page 31)
2 tablespoons honey
¼ cup cider vinegar
1 teaspoon Mustard (page 31)
1 teaspoon celery seed

In a small bowl, mix all of the ingredients until well combined.

FRUITY SPROUT SALAD

4 to 6 servings

3 cups bean sprouts
1 cup chopped pineapple
1 orange, cubed
1 cup (8-ounce can) sliced water
    chestnuts
1 stalk celery, diced
¼ cup sunflower seeds
¼ cup Mayonnaise (page 31)
¼ cup yogurt (page 24)
1 teaspoon honey
1 teaspoon soy sauce
1 teaspoon powdered ginger
¾ teaspoon curry powder
    crisp greens

In a large bowl, toss bean sprouts, pineapple, orange, water chestnuts, celery, and sunflower seeds; chill.

In a separate small bowl, mix mayonnaise, yogurt, honey, soy sauce, ginger, and curry powder; chill.

When ready to serve, toss the fruit and sprout mixture with the dressing. Serve on beds of crisp greens.

GARDEN SALAD WITH CREAMY GARLIC DRESSING

8 servings

1 large head lettuce, torn
4 medium-size carrots, grated
4 radishes, thinly sliced
   Creamy Garlic Dressing (see following recipe)
⅓ cup sunflower seeds

In a large bowl, toss lettuce, carrots, and radishes. Top each serving with Creamy Herb Dressing; garnish with sunflower seeds.

Creamy Garlic Dressing

Yields about 1 cup

½ cup Mayonnaise (page 31)
½ cup buttermilk
1 teaspoon dried parsley flakes
¼ teaspoon garlic powder
¼ teaspoon onion powder
   dash of pepper
   dash of paprika

Combine all ingredients. Cover and refrigerate several hours before serving.

ORIENTAL PEA POD-TOMATO SALAD

4 servings

3 tablespoons cider vinegar
4 teaspoons sesame oil
2 teaspoons soy sauce
½ teaspoon powdered ginger
½ teaspoon sesame seeds
¼ pound fresh pea pods
1 tomato, cut into wedges
   romaine lettuce leaves

In a small bowl or jar, combine vinegar, sesame oil, soy sauce, ginger, and sesame seeds. Set aside.

Remove strings from the pea pods and place in a colander. Blanch by pouring boiling water over the pods. Drain well and allow to cool.

Toss together pea pods and tomato wedges; arrange on romaine leaves on salad plates. Spoon dressing over the vegetables. Serve with additional dressing.

QUICK CAESAR SALAD

6 servings

 6 tablespoons safflower oil
 3 tablespoons lemon juice
 1 clove garlic, minced
 ¼ teaspoon dry mustard
 ¼ teaspoon freshly ground pepper
 2 quarts assorted crisp chilled greens (Boston lettuce, romaine lettuce, and cabbage)
 1 large egg, beaten
 ⅓ cup grated Parmesan or cheddar cheese
 Seasoned Whole Wheat Croutons (page 34)

In a small bowl, combine the oil, lemon juice, garlic, mustard, and pepper. Stir until well blended. Set aside.

To assemble the salad: Tear the greens and place them in a large salad bowl. Pour the dressing over the greens and toss. Pour the egg into the salad and toss again. Add the cheese and Seasoned Whole Wheat Croutons. Toss lightly; serve immediately.

Provide a pepper mill so that each serving can be topped with a fresh grating of pepper.

SPINACH-AVOCADO SALAD WITH LEMON-MUSTARD VINAIGRETTE

6 servings

 2 avocados, peeled and sliced
 ¼ cup lemon juice
 1 pound spinach, torn into pieces
 ½ red onion, thinly sliced
 ⅓ cup sunflower seeds
 Lemon-Mustard Vinaigrette (see following recipe)

Place the avocados in a medium-size bowl and toss with the lemon juice.

Place the spinach in a large salad bowl. Add the avocado slices, onion slices, and sunflower seeds; toss gently. Just before serving, add Lemon-Mustard Vinaigrette and toss again.

Lemon-Mustard Vinaigrette

Yields about ¾ cup

 ½ cup safflower oil
 1½ tablespoons cider vinegar
 3 tablespoons lemon juice
 ¼ teaspoon Mustard (page 31)
 ½ teaspoon freshly ground pepper

Combine all ingredients and mix well. Refrigerate.

SPINACH-APPLE SALAD

4 to 6 servings

⅓ cup Mayonnaise (page 31)
2 tablespoons orange juice
    concentrate
1 pound fresh spinach, torn into
    bite-size pieces
2 red apples, sliced into ½-inch
    wedges

In a small bowl, combine the mayonnaise and orange juice; set aside.

In a large salad bowl, toss the spinach and apple wedges.

Serve in salad bowls; spoon the dressing over each serving. Serve with additional dressing.

SUNSHINE CARROT SALAD

6 servings

3 medium-size carrots, grated
1 cup chopped pineapple
1 medium-size orange, cubed
½ cup raisins
½ cup chopped pecans
¼ cup grated unsweetened coconut
4 tablespoons yogurt (page 24)
    pinch of celery seed
    lettuce or spinach leaves

In a medium-size bowl, toss the carrots, pineapple, orange, raisins, pecans, and coconut.

In a small bowl, mix the yogurt and celery seed. Gently stir into the carrot-and-fruit mixture. Chill 1 to 2 hours.

To serve, place mounds of the mixture on lettuce or spinach leaves.

VEGETABLE SALAD WITH CREAMY HERB DRESSING

2 cups broccoli florets
2 cups cauliflower florets
1½ cups cubed cheddar cheese,
  (6 ounces)
2 stalks celery, sliced
2 carrots, sliced
¼ cucumber, cut into ½-inch cubes
½ green or red pepper, sliced
⅓ cup raisins
  Creamy Herb Dressing (see
  following recipe)
1 cup sunflower seeds

Combine all ingredients except dressing and sunflower seeds; toss well. Refrigerate.

At serving time, place generous portions of the vegetables on salad plates. Lightly spoon on the dressing; garnish each serving with sunflower seeds. Serve with extra dressing.

Creamy Herb Dressing

Yields about 3 cups

1 egg
1 tablespoon cider vinegar
2 tablespoons Mustard (page 31)
1 clove garlic, minced
1 teaspoon dillweed
½ teaspoon dried basil
½ teaspoon dried marjoram
½ teaspoon dried thyme leaves
⅛ teaspoon white pepper
½ cup safflower oil
½ cup buttermilk
2 cups Mayonnaise (page 31)
½ teaspoon celery seed

In a food processor or blender, place egg, vinegar, mustard, garlic, dillweed, basil, marjoram, thyme, and pepper; process until smooth. With machine running, slowly pour in the oil, then the buttermilk, and continue processing until smooth and thick. Transfer to a medium-size bowl and whisk in mayonnaise and celery seed. Refrigerate.

SOUPS

CARAWAY-DILL-POTATO SOUP

6 servings

3 large potatoes, cubed
2 leeks, chopped
1 carrot, grated
1 stalk celery, chopped
3½ cups Vegetable Stock (page 35)
   or water
2 cups half-and-half or milk
1 tablespoon dillweed
½ teaspoon caraway seeds
¼ teaspoon white pepper
3 tablespoons sour cream or sour
   half-and-half
1 egg yolk
6 sprigs parsley

In a Dutch oven or large saucepan, place the potatoes, leeks, carrot, celery, and stock or water; cook until vegetables are tender, about 30 minutes. Add the half-and-half or milk, dill, caraway, and pepper. Simmer the mixture over low heat until it begins to thicken, 15 to 20 minutes.

Just before serving, combine the sour cream or sour half-and-half and the egg yolk. Stir about ¼ cup of the hot soup into this mixture; then pour into the soup pot. Heat through but do not boil.

Garnish each serving with a parsley sprig.

CREAMY TOMATO-VEGETABLE SOUP

4 to 6 servings

1 potato, cut into ½-inch cubes
2 carrots, cut into ½-inch cubes
2 stalks celery, each stalk halved
   and cut into ½-inch slices
1 medium-size onion, chopped
2 bay leaves
1½ teaspoons dried basil
¾ teaspoon dried oregano
¼ teaspoon chili powder
¼ teaspoon pepper
1 cup Vegetable Stock (page 35)
1 16-ounce can tomatoes
2 tablespoons tomato paste
1 cup sour half-and-half or sour
   cream

In a Dutch oven or large saucepan, place the potato, carrots, celery, onion, bay leaves, basil, oregano, chili powder, pepper, and stock. Bring to a boil; reduce heat and simmer, covered, until vegetables are tender, about 10 minutes.

Stir in the tomatoes and tomato paste. Continue to simmer until heated through, about 5 minutes. (Soup may be stored for up to two days at this point.)

Before serving, warm over low heat and gently fold in sour half-and-half or sour cream. Heat through but do not let the soup come to a boil.

PUREED VEGETABLE SOUP WITH WALNUT-CHEESE NUGGETS

2 potatoes, diced
2 medium-size stalks celery, chopped
1 medium-size onion, chopped
1 clove garlic, minced
2 cups Vegetable Stock (page 35)
1 bay leaf
½ teaspoon pepper
½ teaspoon dried thyme leaves, crumbled
4 medium-size carrots, sliced
2 tablespoons butter
½ pound mushrooms, sliced
1 cup milk
1 egg yolk, lightly beaten
1 tablespoon soy sauce
chopped parsley
Walnut-Cheese Nuggets (see following recipe)

In a Dutch oven, place potatoes, celery, onion, garlic, stock, bay leaf, pepper, thyme, and half the carrots. Bring to a boil; lower heat and simmer, covered, until vegetables are very tender, 10 to 15 minutes.

While soup is simmering, in a medium-size saucepan, steam the remaining carrots. In a medium-size skillet, melt the butter and sauté the mushrooms until tender but not brown. Set aside.

When the simmered vegetables are tender, remove the bay leaf and transfer the vegetables and broth to a food processor or blender. Process until smooth. (The soup may be refrigerated at this point and kept for up to 2 days.)

Return the pureed soup mixture to the Dutch oven. Stir in the sautéed mushrooms and steamed carrots; heat. In a measuring cup, combine the milk, egg yolk, and soy sauce. Add to the soup and heat slowly, but do not allow the mixture to boil.

Garnish each serving with a sprinkling of chopped parsley and 3 to 4 Walnut-Cheese Nuggets.

Walnut-Cheese Nuggets

Makes about 25 nuggets

½ cup ground walnuts
½ cup grated cheddar cheese (2 ounces)
1 slice whole wheat bread, torn into cubes
¼ cup toasted wheat germ
2 tablespoons minced onion
¼ cup milk
1 tablespoon chopped fresh parsley
¼ teaspoon pepper
¼ teaspoon dried basil
1 egg, beaten

Preheat oven to 375°F. Oil a 9 × 9-inch baking dish.

In a medium-size bowl, combine all ingredients; roll into 1-inch balls. Arrange in prepared pan. Bake until lightly browned, 25 to 30 minutes.

Walnut-Cheese Nuggets are delicious when served as a soup garnish or appetizer.

SIDE DISHES

MUSHROOM RICE

6 servings

½ pound mushrooms, sliced
2 scallions, chopped
3 tablespoons chopped fresh parsley
2 tablespoons safflower oil
3 cups uncooked brown rice
6 cups Vegetable Stock (page 35)
¼ cup wheat germ
1 tablespoon soy sauce
¼ teaspoon dried basil
¼ teaspoon pepper

In a large skillet, sauté mushrooms, scallions, and parsley in oil until tender; set aside.

In a large saucepan, cook the rice in the stock. (For cooking directions, see page 14.)

Add the rice and remaining ingredients to the mushroom mixture; heat thoroughly, stirring constantly.

ORANGE-TAHINI GREEN BEANS

6 servings

¼ cup butter
1 clove garlic, crushed
¼ cup whole wheat flour
½ cup tahini (sesame butter)
1½ cups orange juice
½ cup water
1 tablespoon soy sauce
3 cups cut green beans, steamed and kept warm
2 tablespoons sesame seeds, toasted

In a medium-size saucepan, melt butter over low heat. Add garlic; stir in flour. Cook, stirring constantly, for 5 minutes. Add tahini, orange juice, water, and soy sauce. Simmer for 10 minutes, stirring frequently.

Spoon hot Orange-Tahini over the warm green beans; sprinkle each serving with sesame seeds. Serve with additional sauce.

MAPLE SQUASH

6 servings

2 pounds acorn squash
2 tablespoons butter
6 tablespoons maple syrup
⅛ teaspoon white pepper
½ cup coarsely chopped walnuts

Preheat oven to 350°F. Coat a 9-inch pie plate or a 1-quart ovenproof casserole with oil.

Cut the squash into ¾-inch chunks. Boil or steam the squash pieces until softened, 10 to 15 minutes. Drain well.

Mash the squash with the butter, 4 tablespoons of the maple syrup, and the pepper. Spoon into the baking dish. Drizzle the remaining maple syrup over the squash. Sprinkle with the walnuts.

Bake until the squash is heated through, about 20 minutes.

TOMATOES PROVENÇAL

6 servings

3 medium-size tomatoes
  freshly ground pepper, to taste
  dash of garlic powder
1½ cups chopped fresh parsley
6 teaspoons wheat germ
1½ teaspoons butter

Preheat oven to 350°F. Oil a 9×9-inch baking pan.

Slice tomatoes into halves; sprinkle each half with freshly ground pepper and garlic powder. On each tomato half, place a ¼-cup mound of parsley. Over this sprinkle 1 teaspoon of wheat germ and dot with ¼ teaspoon butter.

Bake for 25 to 30 minutes.

VEGGIE RICE

6 servings

3 cups cooked brown rice
1 cup peas, cooked
2 tablespoons chopped fresh parsley
2 tablespoons butter
  freshly ground pepper, to taste

In a medium-size saucepan, combine the rice, peas, parsley, and butter. Stir until the mixture is heated through and the butter is melted. Season with pepper.

WALNUT-WILD RICE PILAF

6 servings

1 cup uncooked wild rice
3 cups Vegetable Stock (page 35)
   or water
1 tablespoon finely chopped fresh
   parsley
½ teaspoon dried thyme leaves
½ teaspoon dried marjoram
   freshly ground pepper, to taste
2 tablespoons butter
1 tablespoon soy sauce
½ cup coarsely chopped walnuts

Place the rice in a large saucepan; add enough stock or water to cover rice by 3 inches. Stir in parsley, thyme, and marjoram. Cook over medium heat, uncovered, until rice is tender but not mushy, about 30 minutes. During the cooking period check occasionally to be certain the stock has not cooked away. Add water if necessary.

Drain the rice. Sprinkle with pepper; stir in butter, soy sauce, and walnuts.

BREADS

APPLE-RAISIN BRAN MUFFINS

Makes 24 muffins

2 cups whole wheat flour
1 cup wheat bran
½ cup wheat germ
1½ teaspoons baking soda
½ teaspoon ground nutmeg
½ cup orange juice
1 cup buttermilk or yogurt
   (page 24)
1 egg, beaten
¼ cup molasses
¼ cup maple syrup
¼ cup safflower oil
1 tablespoon grated orange rind
1 cup finely chopped apple
½ cup raisins
½ cup sunflower seeds

Preheat oven to 350°F. Oil enough cups in muffin tins for 24 muffins or line the cups with paper baking cups.

In a large bowl, mix the flour, bran, wheat germ, baking soda, and nutmeg.

In a medium-size bowl, combine orange juice, buttermilk or yogurt, egg, molasses, syrup, and oil. Stir into the dry ingredients; blend well.

Stir in orange rind, apple, raisins, and sunflower seeds. Spoon mixture into prepared muffin tins to ⅔ full. Bake for 20 minutes. Serve with Cinnamon-Honey Butter (page 30).

MIXED GRAIN-HONEY CORN BREAD

Makes 1 loaf

⅓ cup cornmeal
⅓ cup whole wheat flour
⅓ cup wheat germ
1 tablespoon baking powder
2 eggs, beaten
¼ cup safflower oil
¼ cup honey
1 cup buttermilk

Preheat oven to 350°F. Oil a 9-inch round pan.

In a large bowl, combine cornmeal, flour, wheat germ, and baking powder.

In a separate bowl, mix eggs, oil, honey, and buttermilk. Add to the dry ingredients; blend until the dry ingredients are moistened.

Pour into the pan and bake for 35 minutes.

Serve warm; cut into pie-shaped wedges.

This bread is delicious when served with Maple Butter (page 30).

RYE BISCUITS

Makes 12 biscuits

1 cup medium rye flour
1 cup whole wheat pastry flour
1 tablespoon carob powder
2 teaspoons baking powder
½ teaspoon baking soda
6 tablespoons butter, chilled
⅓ cup buttermilk or yogurt
   (page 24)
2 teaspoons molasses
2 teaspoons honey

Preheat oven to 450°F.

In a medium-size bowl, combine the flours, carob powder, baking powder, and baking soda. Cut in butter until mixture resembles coarse crumbs.

In a cup, combine the buttermilk or yogurt, molasses, and honey; add to the flour mixture and stir until evenly moistened. (Dough will be sticky.)

Turn dough out onto a lightly floured work surface and knead 10 to 15 times. With a rolling pin, roll dough into a circle that is ¾-inch thick. Cut out biscuits using a 2-inch round cutter or a glass. Place on baking sheet.

Bake in the preheated oven until lightly browned, about 15 minutes.

Serve warm with Quick Herb Cheese Spread (page 32).

MOLASSES-RYE MUFFINS

Makes 10 muffins

1½ cups rye flour
½ teaspoon baking soda
¼ cup safflower oil
¼ cup molasses
1 egg, beaten
6 tablespoons orange juice
¼ cup golden raisins

Preheat oven to 375°F. Oil enough cups in muffin tins for 10 muffins or line the cups with paper baking cups.

In a large bowl, combine flour and baking soda; mix well.

In a small bowl, beat the oil, molasses, egg, and orange juice. Add to flour mixture; add raisins, stirring enough only to moisten the dry ingredients.

Spoon the batter into the muffin tins. Bake for 20 minutes. Serve warm with Orange-Honey Butter (page 29).

WHOLE WHEAT-ORANGE TOAST

Makes 32 slices

3 cups whole wheat pastry flour
1 teaspoon baking powder
4 eggs
1 cup safflower oil
¾ cup honey
2 teaspoons grated orange rind
1 teaspoon vanilla extract
½ cup chopped walnuts

Preheat oven to 325°F. Oil 2 loaf pans, 8½ × 4½-inches.

In a large bowl, combine flour and baking powder.

In a medium-size bowl, beat the eggs, oil, honey, orange rind, and vanilla. Add to ingredients; blend thoroughly. Stir in the nuts.

Spoon into the loaf pans. Bake until the loaves spring back when lightly touched in their centers and are golden brown, 40 to 45 minutes.

Remove loaves from pans and cool on a wire rack. Cut into ½-inch slices. Place on ungreased baking sheets. Toast in a 325°F oven until golden brown on underside, 12 to 15 minutes. Turn slices and toast until opposite side is golden, 10 to 12 minutes. Cool slices on a wire rack. Store in plastic bags or covered containers.

DESSERTS

APPLE CRISP

Makes 9 squares

5 medium-size baking apples
   juice of 1 lemon
⅓ cup whole wheat flour
1 teaspoon ground cinnamon
½ cup raisins
2 tablespoons butter
2 tablespoons honey
1 cup rolled oats
½ cup whole walnuts
¼ cup sunflower seeds
¼ teaspoon ground allspice
½ cup orange juice or apple juice

Preheat oven to 375°F. Oil a 9 × 9-inch baking pan.

Slice the apples; place in a medium-size bowl; drizzle with lemon juice and toss together with 1 tablespoon flour, ½ teaspoon cinnamon, and raisins. Set aside.

In a medium-size saucepan melt the butter and honey. Remove from the heat and stir in the oats, remaining flour, walnuts, sunflower seeds, remaining cinnamon, and allspice.

Place ½ of the apple mixture in the baking pan. Spread ½ of the oat mixture onto the apples. Repeat layers. Pour juice over the top.

Bake uncovered 35 to 40 minutes. Cover if the top begins to brown too quickly. Serve at room temperature; cut into 3-inch squares just before serving.

Apple Crisp is delicious served warm with yogurt (page 24).

APRICOT WHIP

6 servings

1¼ cups dried apricots
1¼ cups yogurt (page 24)
2 tablespoons honey
2 tablespoons chopped pecans

Cover apricots with hot water and soak for 30 minutes. Drain well.

In a food processor or blender, combine the apricots, yogurt, and honey. Process until smooth. Chill.

To serve, sprinkle nuts on each portion.

BAKED APPLES IN ORANGE SAUCE

6 servings

6 medium-size baking apples
⅓ cup minced raisins
⅓ cup finely chopped almonds
½ cup maple syrup
½ cup orange juice
3 tablespoons butter
2 teaspoons grated orange rind
¼ teaspoon ground nutmeg
2 cups yogurt (page 24)

Preheat oven to 375°F. Core apples to within ½ inch of bottoms.

Combine raisins and almonds; spoon the mixture into the apple centers.

Set the apples in a shallow baking dish that is just large enough to accommodate them and 1 cup of liquid.

In a small saucepan, heat the syrup, juice, and butter. When the butter has melted, add the orange rind and nutmeg, stirring until blended. Pour this mixture over and around the apples.

Bake, basting often, until apples are tender, about 40 minutes.

Serve the warm apples in bowls. Top each with yogurt and drizzle with the sauce that has accumulated in the baking pan.

CAROB CREME PATISSERIE

6 servings

½ cup carob powder
½ cup water
6 egg yolks
½ cup honey
½ cup whole wheat pastry flour, sifted
1½ cups milk
2 tablespoons butter
1 tablespoon vanilla extract

In a small saucepan, combine the carob powder and water; stir until smooth. Bring to a boil over very low heat, stirring constantly, for about 2 minutes. Set aside to cool.

Place yolks in a medium-size saucepan. Beat in the honey, then the flour. Stir until completely smooth. Add milk gradually, stirring again until completely smooth. Place over low heat and simmer until mixture thickens, stirring constantly. Remove from heat; add carob sauce, butter, and vanilla. Stir until butter has melted. Chill.

This pudding is very rich; serve in small portions.

BAKED BANANAS WITH RAISIN-WALNUT SAUCE

6 to 8 servings

4 medium-size bananas
4 tablespoons honey
1 tablespoon lemon juice
¼ teaspoon ground nutmeg
4 tablespoons butter
    Raisin-Walnut Sauce (see
    following recipe)

Preheat oven to 350°F. Oil a 9 × 9-inch baking pan.

Peel the bananas and cut into halves lengthwise, then again crosswise. Arrange the banana quarters in the pan with the uncut sides up.

In a small bowl, combine the honey and lemon juice; brush over the bananas with a pastry brush. Sprinkle with nutmeg; dot the bananas with butter.

Bake until tender but not mushy, about 10 minutes. While the bananas are baking, prepare the Raisin-Walnut Sauce. Pour the hot Raisin-Walnut Sauce over the bananas. Serve immediately.

Raisin-Walnut Sauce

Yields about ¾ cup

½ cup golden raisins
½ cup chopped pecans
½ cup orange juice

Combine all ingredients in a medium-size saucepan; simmer over medium heat until raisins are puffed, about 10 minutes.

BANANA FROZEN YOGURT

4 servings

4 medium-size bananas
1 cup yogurt (page 24)
2 tablespoons honey

Peel bananas, wrap in a plastic bag, and freeze overnight.

At serving time, cut the bananas into 1-inch slices while still frozen. Place the yogurt and honey in a food processor or blender; process until combined. Gradually add the banana slices, and continue to blend until smooth.

Spoon into dessert cups. Serve immediately.

Banana Frozen Yogurt is delicious topped with fresh blueberries or strawberries.

CAROB-PINEAPPLE CREAM

1 cup cold water
1 tablespoon vanilla extract
½ cup nonfat dry milk
1 tablespoon safflower oil
1 cup crushed pineapple, drained
2 tablespoons carob powder
2 tablespoons honey
6 tablespoons finely chopped pecans

Pour water and vanilla into a food processor or blender; process. While the machine continues to run, gradually add dry milk, oil, pineapple, carob powder, and honey. Blend well.

Pour mixture into freezer tray and freeze.

Let stand at room temperature for 15 minutes before serving. Garnish each serving with 1 tablespoon pecans.

HONEY-PUMPKIN MOUSSE

3 teaspoons unflavored gelatin
6 tablespoons water
4 egg yolks, beaten
4 tablespoons honey
1 cup mashed pumpkin
½ teaspoon ground cinnamon
¼ teaspoon ground allspice
¼ teaspoon ground nutmeg
1 cup heavy cream
1 teaspoon honey
   ground nutmeg

Sprinkle the gelatin over water in top of a double boiler and let stand until softened. Place over simmering water and stir until gelatin is completely dissolved.

In a medium-size bowl, beat egg yolks until thick and lemon-colored. Stir in honey. Add pumpkin, cinnamon, allspice, and nutmeg; fold in. Stir in the gelatin-water mixture.

In a small bowl, whip ¾ cup heavy cream until soft peaks form. Gently fold into the pumpkin mixture.

Spoon the mousse into serving cups; chill thoroughly.

Whip the remaining cream until soft peaks form; beat in the honey.

To serve, garnish each portion with a dollop of the sweetened whipped cream and top with a sprinkling of nutmeg.

FRESH FRUIT FONDUE

6 to 8 servings

2 cups yogurt (page 24)
⅔ cup orange juice concentrate
6 cups assorted fresh fruit (apples,
    bananas, oranges, pears,
    pineapple, and strawberries)
    cut into ½-inch cubes
3 tablespoons lemon juice

In a small bowl, combine the yogurt and the orange juice concentrate. Cover and refrigerate.

In a large bowl, toss the fruit, and stir in the lemon juice. Refrigerate.

At serving time, arrange the fruit on a platter, surrounding the bowl of the orange yogurt. Provide guests with skewers to dip the fruit into the yogurt. Or, serve the fruit in dessert bowls with the orange yogurt poured over the top of each portion.

FROZEN APRICOT-ORANGE MOUSSE

6 servings

1 cup dried apricots
3 tablespoons orange juice
¼ cup honey
2 egg whites
½ cup heavy cream
½ teaspoon vanilla extract
1 tablespoon grated orange rind

In a medium-size saucepan, cover the apricots with water, and cook until they are very soft, about 30 minutes. Drain.

Place the apricots, orange juice, and honey in a food processor or blender and process until smooth.

Beat the egg whites until stiff; carefully fold in the apricot puree.

Whip the cream until it forms peaks; beat in the vanilla. Fold the whipped cream and orange rind into the apricot mixture.

Spoon the mousse into a 1-quart soufflé dish or 6 dessert cups. Freeze for 4 to 6 hours before serving.

HONEY-CARROT CAKE WITH KEFIR CHEESE FROSTING

Makes 1 cake

2 cups whole wheat flour
2 teaspoons baking soda
1 teaspoon ground cinnamon
½ teaspoon ground allspice
1 cup honey
4 eggs
1 cup safflower oil
3 cups finely grated carrots
1 cup coarsely chopped walnuts or pecans
Kefir Cheese Frosting (see following recipe)

Preheat oven to 375°F. Coat with oil a sheet pan, 13 × 9-inches or 2 round pans 9 inches in diameter.

In a large bowl, combine flour, baking soda, cinnamon, and allspice.

In a separate bowl, mix honey, eggs, and oil. Add to the dry mixture and stir until well blended.

Add carrots and nuts; stir until evenly distributed.

Pour into prepared pan or pans. Bake 40 to 45 minutes for the large sheet, or 30 to 35 minutes for the layers. Cool on a rack.

Frost the cake with Kefir Cheese Frosting. For the large cake, frost in the pan and cut into squares to serve. For the 9-inch pans, remove layers from the pans after they have cooled. Assemble and frost as a layer cake.

Store the cake in the refrigerator until serving time.

Kefir Cheese Frosting

Yields about 1½ cups

1½ cups kefir cheese or cream cheese, softened (12 ounces)
3 tablespoons honey
2 tablespoons butter, at room temperature
¼ cup nonfat dry milk
1 to 3 tablespoons orange juice
1 tablespoon toasted wheat germ

In a small bowl, beat the cheese, honey, and butter until light and fluffy. Beat in the dry milk. Beat in 1 tablespoon orange juice, or more if necessary to achieve spreading consistency.

Spread the frosting on the cake. Sprinkle wheat germ over the top.

MAPLE-SAUCED ORANGES

6 oranges
½ cup orange juice
¼ cup maple syrup
¼ cup slivered almonds

6 servings

Peel the oranges, cut into 1-inch cubes and place in a medium-size serving bowl.

In a separate small bowl, combine the orange juice and the syrup. Pour this mixture over the oranges. Chill at least 1 hour.

At serving time, top with almonds.

MAPLE-YOGURT GINGERBREAD WITH HONEY-LEMON SAUCE

2 cups whole wheat flour
¼ cup wheat germ
2 teaspoons baking powder
1 teaspoon baking soda
1 teaspoon powdered ginger
½ teaspoon ground cinnamon
¼ teaspoon ground cloves
⅓ cup safflower oil
½ cup maple syrup
½ cup molasses
½ cup yogurt (page 24)
2 eggs, beaten
   Honey-Lemon Sauce (see
      following recipe) or Apricot-
      Orange Sauce (page 53)
   freshly ground nutmeg
½ cup finely chopped pecans

Makes 1 cake or 18 cupcakes

Preheat oven to 350°F. Oil a 9 × 9-inch baking pan or cups in muffin tins for 18 cupcakes (or line the cups with paper baking cups).

In a medium-size bowl, combine the flour, wheat germ, baking powder, baking soda, ginger, cinnamon, and cloves.

In a small bowl, combine the oil, syrup, molasses, yogurt, and eggs. Add to the dry mixture and stir until well blended.

Pour into the baking pan; bake until cake springs back when lightly touched in the center, about 30 minutes. (Bake cupcakes for 20 to 25 minutes.)

Serve warm with Honey-Lemon Sauce or Apricot-Orange Sauce. Garnish each serving with a grating of nutmeg and chopped pecans.

Honey-Lemon Sauce

2 tablespoons cornstarch
1½ cups water
⅓ cup honey
1 egg, beaten
¼ cup lemon juice
2 teaspoons grated lemon rind
1 tablespoon butter
   dash of nutmeg

Yields about 2 cups

In a medium-size saucepan, mix the cornstarch with a small amount of the water; stir until dissolved. Add the remaining water, honey, and egg; blend well. Cook over medium heat, stirring constantly, until the mixture comes to a boil. Remove the pan from the heat. Stir in the lemon juice, lemon rind, butter, and nutmeg.

Serve warm over Maple-Yogurt Gingerbread.

SPICY APPLE CAKE WITH ORANGE-RAISIN SAUCE

Makes 1 cake

1⅔ cups whole wheat flour
2 teaspoons baking powder
1 teaspoon ground cinnamon
¼ teaspoon ground allspice
¼ teaspoon ground cloves
3 eggs, separated
⅔ cup safflower oil
⅓ cup honey
½ teaspoon vanilla extract
2 medium-size apples, minced
½ cup raisins
½ cup chopped walnuts
Orange-Raisin Sauce (see following recipe)

Preheat oven to 350°F. Oil a 9 × 9-inch baking pan.

In a large bowl, mix flour, baking powder, cinnamon, allspice, and cloves.

In a small bowl, beat egg yolks. Add oil, honey, and vanilla; mix well. Stir in apples, raisins, and walnuts. Add to the flour mixture; stir well.

In a medium-size bowl, beat the egg whites until stiff but not dry. Fold carefully into the cake batter; do not overmix.

Pour into the baking pan. Bake until a toothpick comes out clean when inserted in the center, 35 to 40 minutes.

Serve warm, and top each serving with warm Orange-Raisin Sauce.

Orange-Raisin Sauce

Yields about 2 cups

2 cups orange juice
¼ cup honey
1 tablespoon butter
¼ cup raisins
2 tablespoons cornstarch
2 tablespoons water

In a medium-size saucepan, place the orange juice and honey; bring to a simmer over medium heat. Stir in the butter and raisins; continue to simmer, stirring until butter has melted. Reduce heat.

Dissolve the cornstarch in the water. Stir into the mixture in the saucepan and simmer over low heat, stirring constantly, until thick, about 3 minutes.

PINEAPPLE FROST

2 cups crushed pineapple, drained
⅓ cup orange juice concentrate
⅓ cup chopped pecans

In a medium-size bowl, combine the pineapple with the orange juice concentrate; mix well. Pour into a freezer container and cover. Freeze several hours.

To serve, spoon into dessert bowls and garnish each serving with 1 tablespoon chopped pecans.

If the mixture freezes solid, let it stand at room temperature for 15 to 20 minutes before serving.

Elegant Evenings

An elegant dinner for a few friends may be a muti-coursed affair, but need not to be complicated to prepare. Most important, the food and presentation must always be special. I feel that the key to success is organization. When a dinner party is well orchestrated, both you and your guests can relax and enjoy the occasion to the fullest. You can arrange the meal in a way that permits you to be with your guests as much as possible, and to participate in a leisurely dining experience.

I seize every opportunity to use imaginative table decor as a way to spark conversation and add a festive note to my dinner parties. Even the smallest creative touches are likely to be noticed and commented upon by friends.

MENUS
ELEGANT EVENINGS

ɣ Menton Soup
   Whole Wheat Crescent Rolls
   Spinach-Pine Nut Salad with Tahini-Poppy Seed Dressing
   French Apple Tart

ɣ Orange-Carrot Soup
   Romaine-Cashew Salad
   Many-Grain Maple Muffins
   Cheesy Garden Casserole
   Carob Chiffon Pie with Honey-Coconut Crust

ɣ Zucchini Soup with Toasted Cheese Cubes
   Orange-Almond Salad with Honey-Poppy Seed Dressing
   Cauli-Broc Quiche in Whole Wheat-Sesame Crust
   Sautéed Cherry Tomatoes
   Whole Wheat Puffs with Orange-Honey Ice and Hot Carob Sauce

ɣ Asparagus-Leek Soup
   Herbed Muffins
   Winter Salad with Green French Dressing
   Potato and Cheese Bake
   Sesame Green Beans
   Raspberry Trifle

Y Carrot-Onion Soup with Tiny Puffs
Avocado-Almond Salad with Apricot-Yogurt Dressing
Garden Vegetable Crepes with Cheese and Mushroom Sauces
Honey-Lemon Chiffon Pie with Carob Chip Crumb Crust

Y Tossed Vegetable and Apple Salad with Avocado Dressing
Vegetable Tartlets with Sesame-Soy Crust
Cheese-Buttermilk Soufflé
Carob-Pecan Torte

Y Vegetable Egg Rolls with Apricot Sweet-and-Sour Sauce and Hot Mustard
      Sauce
Chinese Watercress Soup
Oriental Sprout Salad with Sesame-Soy Dressing
Vegetable Stir-Fry
Fried Rice and Tofu
Pineapple-Coconut Sherbet
Whole Wheat-Almond Cookies

MAIN COURSES

CAULI-BROC QUICHE IN WHOLE WHEAT-SESAME CRUST

6 servings

1 Whole Wheat-Sesame Crust (see following recipe)
¼ pound mushrooms, sliced
2 tablespoons butter
2 cups cauliflower florets
2 cups broccoli florets
3 eggs
1½ cups half-and-half or cream
1 tablespoon chopped fresh parsley
1 tablespoon soy sauce
¼ teaspoon dried basil
¼ teaspoon dried summer savory
¼ teaspoon dried tarragon
¼ teaspoon dried thyme
  dash of white pepper
2 scallions, chopped
1 cup cubed colby cheese (4 ounces)
  paprika

Preheat oven to 375°F. Prepare the Whole Wheat-Sesame Crust. Set aside.

In a medium-size skillet, melt the butter and sauté the mushrooms until tender; drain.

In a large saucepan, steam the cauliflower and broccoli until crisp-tender.

In a small bowl, lightly beat the eggs; stir in the half-and-half or cream, parsley, soy sauce, basil, summer savory, tarragon, thyme, and pepper.

In a large bowl, toss the mushrooms, cauliflower, broccoli, and scallions; spread in prepared crust. Arrange the cheese cubes evenly on the top. Pour on the cream mixture; sprinkle with paprika.

Bake until set, 30 to 40 minutes.

If desired, the crust, vegetables, and cream sauce can each be prepared in advance. Assemble and bake the quiche just before serving time.

Whole Wheat-Sesame Crust

Makes 1 crust

1¼ cups whole wheat flour
¼ cup sesame seeds
¼ cup safflower oil
5 to 6 tablespoons cold water

Preheat oven to 375°F.

In a large bowl, mix flour and sesame seeds. Add the oil, a drop at a time, mixing constantly with a fork, until the mixture resembles a bowl of crumbs. Add water, 1 tablespoon at a time, mixing well between additions until mixture forms a firm ball. Turn onto a work surface and roll out between sheets of waxed paper. Fit into a 9-inch pie plate; flute the edges. Prick the bottom and sides with a fork.

Bake for 12 minutes.

If preferred, this crust may be pressed into the pie plate.

CHEESE-BUTTERMILK SOUFFLÉ

4 servings

¼ cup grated Parmesan cheese
  (1 ounce)
2 tablespoons butter
4 tablespoons whole wheat flour
1⅓ cups buttermilk
5 eggs, separated
1 cup grated cheddar cheese
  (4 ounces)
¼ teaspoon dry mustard
1 tablespoon grated onion
  dash of pepper
  pinch of cream of tartar

Preheat oven to 350°F. Lightly butter the bottom and sides of a 1½-quart soufflé dish; dust with Parmesan cheese.

In a medium-size saucepan, melt the butter; add the flour and stir until bubbly. Gradually pour in the buttermilk; continue cooking until the mixture is smooth and thick.

Beat the egg yolks well. Stir ¼ cup of the sauce into the yolks; pour into the saucepan; add the cheddar cheese. Cook, stirring constantly, until the cheese melts and the mixture is smooth. Stir in the mustard, onion, and pepper; cool.

Beat the egg whites with the cream of tartar until stiff; fold gently into the cheese mixture. Spoon into the soufflé dish.

Bake for 25 to 30 minutes. A knife inserted in the center will come out clean when the soufflé is done. Serve immediately.

CHEESY GARDEN CASSEROLE

6 servings

1 tablespoon butter
½ cup slivered almonds
2 cups cooked brown rice
¼ cup chopped fresh parsley
2 tablespoons soy sauce
2 cups sliced broccoli
4 carrots, cut into julienne strips
1 zucchini, cut into julienne strips
1 cup cut green beans
1 cup cauliflower florets
2 cups Marinara Sauce (page 188)
  or tomato sauce
1 cup shredded colby cheese
  (4 ounces)
1 cup shredded Monterey Jack
  cheese (4 ounces)

Preheat oven to 375°F. Oil a 10×8-inch covered baking dish or a 1-quart ovenproof casserole with cover.

In a small skillet, melt butter; sauté slivered almonds until lightly browned. Add to cooked rice; stir in parsley and soy sauce. Spread rice mixture on the bottom of the baking dish.

Steam the vegetables until crisp-tender, 5 to 7 minutes. Spoon the vegetables over the rice and pour the marinara sauce evenly over the top.

Cover the baking dish and bake until heated through, about 30 minutes. Combine the cheeses; sprinkle over the casserole. Return the dish to the oven, uncovered, until the cheeses melt, about 5 minutes.

For variety, use other vegetables.

GARDEN VEGETABLE CREPES WITH CHEESE AND MUSHROOM SAUCES

6 to 8 servings

¼ cup butter
2 tablespoons chopped onion
1 clove garlic, crushed
½ cup wheat germ
1 tablespoon chopped fresh parsley
⅛ teaspoon pepper
¼ teaspoon dried thyme leaves
¼ teaspoon dried marjoram
2 tablespoons soy sauce
2 hard-cooked eggs, finely chopped
1 cup chopped cooked carrots
1 cup chopped cooked cauliflower
1 cup chopped cooked broccoli
Wheat Germ Crepes (see accompanying recipe)
Cheese Sauce (see accompanying recipe)
Mushroom Sauce (see accompanying recipe)
paprika
parsley sprigs

Make Wheat Germ Crepes; set aside.
Preheat oven to 350°F.

In a large saucepan or Dutch oven, melt the butter; add onion, garlic, and wheat germ. Cook over medium heat, stirring constantly, until onion is softened and wheat germ is light brown. Add parsley, pepper, thyme, marjoram, and soy sauce; stir well. Gently toss in eggs, carrots, cauliflower, and broccoli.

Spoon the filling onto crepes and roll. Line rolled crepes closely together on ovenproof platters. Bake until crepes are hot but not dry, 15 to 20 minutes.

To serve, place two crepes on each plate. Spoon Cheese Sauce over one and Mushroom Sauce on the other.

Garnish each serving with a sprinkling of paprika and a sprig of parsley.

Wheat Germ Crepes

Makes 16 to 18 crepes

3 eggs
1 cup whole wheat flour
¼ cup wheat germ
1 cup milk
½ cup water

Place all ingredients in food processor or blender; process until smooth, about 1 minute. Pour crepe batter into a small bowl or jar, cover, and refrigerate at least 1 hour.

Lightly oil a traditional crepe pan or a small skillet. Heat pan over medium-high heat. Stir the crepe batter and pour a scant ¼ cup into pan. Tilt pan to spread batter evenly over the surface. Cook until crepe is light brown; then turn and brown opposite side. Repeat until all batter is used. Stack finished crepes on a platter.

The crepes may be made a day before serving. After making the crepes, cool them, then stack between sheets of waxed paper. Store in the refrigerator. Bring the crepes to room temperature before filling.

Cheese Sauce

2 tablespoons butter
2 tablespoons whole wheat flour
1 cup milk
1 cup grated cheddar cheese
   (4 ounces)
1 teaspoon dry mustard
½ teaspoon Worcestershire sauce
⅛ teaspoon white pepper

Melt butter in medium-size saucepan over low heat; remove from heat and blend in flour. Return to medium heat and cook, stirring constantly, until mixture is smooth and bubbly. Remove from heat again; stir in milk. Return to medium heat, stirring constantly, until mixture is thick and smooth. Do not allow the mixture to boil. Add cheese, mustard, Worcestershire, and pepper, stirring constantly, until the cheese has melted.

Mushroom Sauce

Yields about 1⅓ cups

4 tablespoons butter
1 pound fresh mushrooms,
   coarsely chopped
4 tablespoons whole wheat flour
1⅓ cups milk
1 tablespoon lemon juice
   dash of ground nutmeg
   dash of white pepper

In a medium-size saucepan, melt butter over low heat; stir in mushrooms and sauté until tender. Reduce heat; add flour, and stir until mixture is smooth. Remove from heat; gradually stir in the milk. Return to medium heat, stirring constantly, until mixture is thick and smooth. Do not allow the mixture to boil. Stir in the lemon juice, nutmeg, and pepper. Taste and add more seasonings, if desired.

POTATO AND CHEESE BAKE

4 to 6 servings

2 large potatoes
1 cup grated cheddar cheese
   (4 ounces)
2 scallions, chopped
2 eggs
1 cup cottage cheese (8 ounces)
4 tablespoons chopped fresh parsley
   pepper, to taste

Cut potatoes into thirds and simmer just until tender, 15 to 20 minutes. Drain, cool partially, and cut into ¼-inch-thick slices.

Preheat oven to 375°F. Oil a 9×9-inch baking dish.

In the dish, layer ½ of the potatoes, followed by ½ of the cheddar, and ½ of the scallions. Repeat layers.

In a food processor or blender, process the eggs and cottage cheese until smooth. Stir in 2 tablespoons of the chopped parsley and pepper. Pour this sauce over the potatoes. Sprinkle remaining parsley over the top.

Bake until top is lightly browned, 20 to 30 minutes.

VEGETABLE STIR-FRY

6 servings

8 dried black mushrooms
½ cup Vegetable Stock (page 35)
2 tablespoons cornstarch
1 tablespoon soy sauce
⅛ teaspoon white pepper
2 scallions
3 tablespoons safflower oil
2 teaspoons finely grated peeled
    ginger root
1 clove garlic, minced
½ cup sliced water chestnuts
1 stalk celery, chopped
½ cup bamboo shoots
½ pound pea pods, blanched
1 large tomato, cut into 12 wedges

Soak the mushrooms in warm water until soft, about 30 minutes. Clean with a soft brush to remove any sandy particles. Coarsely chop; set aside.

In a cup, combine stock, cornstarch, soy sauce, and pepper; set aside.

Slice the scallion tops into matchstick strips. Immerse in cold water to form curls; set aside.

In a wok or large skillet, heat the oil. Add the ginger and garlic; stir-fry quickly. Stir in mushrooms, water chestnuts, celery, and bamboo shoots; stir-fry about 1 minute. Add the stock mixture; stir until evenly distributed. Mix in the pea pods and tomato; stir until the mixture is heated through.

Spread the Garden Vegetable Stir-Fry on a serving platter. Garnish with scallion curls. Serve immediately.

SALADS

AVOCADO-ALMOND SALAD WITH APRICOT-YOGURT DRESSING

8 servings

2 tablespoons butter
½ cup slivered almonds
1 large head romaine lettuce, torn
½ pound spinach, torn
1 cup mung bean sprouts
2 avocados, each sliced into eight
    pieces
  Apricot-Yogurt Dressing (see
    following recipe)

In a small skillet, melt butter; sauté almonds in butter; set aside to cool.

In a large salad bowl, toss romaine, spinach, and sprouts. Divide onto salad plates. Place 2 avocado slices on each serving; top with Apricot-Yogurt Dressing. Garnish each serving with almonds.

Apricot-Yogurt Dressing

Yields about 1¼ cups

1 cup yogurt (page 24)
¼ cup coarsely chopped dried
    apricots
3 tablespoons safflower oil
2 tablespoons cider vinegar
1 tablespoon honey
1 teaspoon minced onion
1 teaspoon celery seed
⅛ teaspoon dry mustard
    dash of freshly ground pepper

In a food processor or blender, blend yogurt and apricots until mixture is smooth. Stir in oil, vinegar, honey, onion, celery seed, mustard, and pepper. Chill briefly before serving.

ORANGE-ALMOND SALAD WITH HONEY-POPPY SEED DRESSING

6 servings

⅓ cup slivered almonds
1 tablespoon butter
1 head romaine lettuce, leaves
    broken
⅓ cup raisins
1 orange, cubed
1 stalk celery, chopped
1 cup alfalfa sprouts
    Honey-Poppy Seed Dressing (see
    following recipe)

In a small skillet, sauté the almonds in the butter. Set aside to cool.

In a large salad bowl, toss the romaine, raisins, orange, celery, sprouts, and almonds.

Serve with Honey-Poppy Seed Dressing.

Honey-Poppy Seed Dressing

Yields 1¾ cups

½ cup cider vinegar
¾ cup safflower oil
½ cup honey
2 tablespoons poppy seeds
½ teaspoon minced dried onion
¼ teaspoon pepper

Combine all ingredients in a medium-size bowl; refrigerate. Serve over Orange-Almond Salad.

ORIENTAL SPROUT SALAD WITH SESAME-SOY DRESSING

6 servings

8 leaves red-leaf lettuce, torn into
    bite-size pieces
1½ cups alfalfa sprouts
1½ cups bean sprouts
¾ cup slivered almonds
½ cup chopped scallions
2 oranges, cubed
    Sesame-Soy Dressing (see
    following recipe)

In a large salad bowl, toss all ingredients except the dressing. Chill.

Toss again with Sesame-Soy Dressing just before serving.

Sesame-Soy Dressing

Yields about ½ cup

3 teaspoons soy sauce
¾ teaspoon powdered ginger
4 tablespoons cider vinegar
6 teaspoons sesame oil

In a small bowl, blend the soy sauce and ginger. Stir in the vinegar and sesame oil. Serve on Oriental Sprout Salad.

ROMAINE-CASHEW SALAD

6 to 8 servings

⅓ cup safflower oil
¼ cup cider vinegar
1 tablespoon Mustard (page 31)
¼ teaspoon freshly ground pepper
⅛ teaspoon ground cumin
⅛ teaspoon ground cardamom
1 head romaine lettuce
1 cup cashews
¼ cup sliced red onion
½ cup cooked chick-peas, chilled

In a small bowl or jar, combine oil, vinegar, mustard, pepper, cumin, and cardamom. Blend well; taste and increase seasonings, if desired. Set aside.

Break romaine leaves into a large salad bowl. Add cashews, onion, and chick-peas; toss.

Before serving, pour desired amount of oil-vinegar dressing over salad. Toss lightly; serve immediately.

SPINACH-PINE NUT SALAD WITH TAHINI-POPPY SEED DRESSING

8 servings

2   tablespoons butter
½   cup pine nuts
½   pound spinach, torn
1   head romaine lettuce, torn
1   pound mushrooms, sliced
    Tahini-Poppy Seed Dressing (see
       following recipe)

In a small skillet, melt butter; sauté the pine nuts; set aside to cool.

In a large bowl, toss the spinach, romaine, mushrooms, and pine nuts. Serve with Tahini-Poppy Seed Dressing.

Tahini-Poppy Seed Dressing

Yields about 2 cups

¾   cup tahini (sesame butter)
¾   cup cider vinegar
¾   cup safflower oil
¼   cup water
4   tablespoons honey
1   tablespoon poppy seeds

Whisk together all ingredients. Cover and refrigerate. If very thick, add more water before serving.

This dressing also makes a delicious dip for raw vegetables.

WINTER SALAD WITH GREEN FRENCH DRESSING

6 servings

2   cups shredded red cabbage
2   large carrots, grated
4   stalks celery, thinly sliced
1   cup thinly sliced cauliflower florets
2   stalks broccoli, thinly sliced
6   broccoli florets
    Green French Dressing (see
       following recipe)

In a large bowl, toss the cabbage, carrots, celery, cauliflower, and sliced broccoli. Garnish with broccoli florets.

Serve with Green French Dressing.

Green French Dressing

Yields about 1 cup

¾   cup safflower oil
½   cup parsley sprigs
3   tablespoons cider vinegar
1   teaspoon Mustard (page 31)
⅛   teaspoon pepper
    dash of cayenne pepper

Place all ingredients in a food processor or blender; process until smooth.

TOSSED VEGETABLE AND APPLE SALAD WITH AVOCADO DRESSING

4 servings

1 head lettuce, torn
1 medium-size zucchini, cut into ½-inch cubes
1 red pepper, cut into ½-inch pieces
2 stalks celery, cut into ½-inch slices
1 apple, cut into ½-inch cubes
  Avocado Dressing (see following recipe)

In a large bowl, toss lettuce, zucchini, red pepper, celery, and apple. Serve with Avocado Dressing.

Avocado Dressing

Yields about 1 cup

1 medium-size avocado, cubed
½ cup yogurt (page 24)
5 tablespoons lemon juice
2 tablespoons safflower oil
¼ cup chopped green pepper
1 scallion, chopped
1 clove garlic, minced
¼ teaspoon pepper
  few drops of hot pepper sauce

In a food processor or blender, process all ingredients until smooth; refrigerate at least 1 hour to blend flavors.

SOUPS

ASPARAGUS-LEEK SOUP

4 to 6 servings

4 tablespoons butter
3 cups sliced mushrooms
3 leeks, sliced
1½ pounds asparagus, cut into 1-inch pieces
2 cups Vegetable Stock (page 35)
3 tablespoons whole wheat flour
2 cups half-and-half or milk
2 cups cooked corn
¼ to ½ teaspoon curry powder
  dash of white pepper

In a large saucepan or Dutch oven, melt the butter; sauté the mushrooms and leeks until tender but not browned. Remove pan from heat; set aside.

In a medium-size saucepan, cook the asparagus in the stock until tender.

Stir in the flour into the sautéed mushrooms and leeks. Pour in the stock and asparagus; stir until smooth. Add the half-and-half or milk, corn, curry, and pepper.

Simmer, stirring frequently, until smooth and thick; do not boil. Serve hot.

CARROT-ONION SOUP WITH TINY PUFFS

6 to 8 servings

    3 tablespoons butter
4 to 5 medium-size carrots, grated
    1 medium-size onion, chopped
    1 tablespoon honey
    ⅓ cup uncooked brown rice
    4 cups Vegetable Stock (page 35)
    ½ teaspoon dillweed
    1 cup hot milk
      Tiny Puffs (see following recipe)

In a Dutch oven, melt butter over medium heat; add the carrots and onion; sauté about 5 minutes. Add the honey and stir until vegetables are coated. Stir in the rice, stock, and dillweed. Cover, reduce heat to low, and cook until rice is well done, about 45 minutes.

Ladle about ½ of the soup mixture into a food processor or blender; puree. Return to Dutch oven. (At this point, the soup may be stored for 1 day in the refrigerator, if desired.)

Before serving, heat soup and stir in the hot milk. Heat thoroughly but do not boil.

Serve with Tiny Puffs.

Tiny Puffs

Makes 24 puffs

    1 tablespoon butter
    ¼ cup boiling water
    ¼ cup whole wheat pastry flour
    1 egg

Preheat oven to 400°F. Line a baking sheet with aluminum foil.

Place butter and water in a medium-size saucepan. Bring to a rolling boil over medium heat, but do not allow to evaporate.

Add the flour; stir vigorously. Cook, stirring constantly, until mixture forms a ball that does not separate, about 1 minute. Remove from heat and cool slightly.

Add egg and beat vigorously until mixture is smooth.

Drop ½-teaspoon portions 1 inch apart onto baking sheet.

Bake in 400°F oven for 15 minutes; then reduce oven temperature to 350°F and continue baking until tops are lightly browned and crispy, about 10 minutes.

Remove puffs from the sheet with a spatula. Make a small slit in the side of each to allow the steam to escape.

Cool puffs on a wire rack. To preserve crispness, store in a paper bag until ready to use. These puffs are best when made the day you plan to use them.

CHINESE WATERCRESS SOUP

6 servings

5 cups Vegetable Stock (page 35)
2 tablespoons soy sauce
1 teaspoon finely grated peeled
   ginger root
½ teaspoon honey
⅛ teasppon white pepper
¾ cup watercress leaves
2 tablespoons minced scallion

In a 1½-quart saucepan, combine the stock, soy sauce, ginger, honey, and pepper. Simmer, covered, for 15 minutes. Bring to a full boil; add watercress and green onions. Cover, reduce heat, and simmer 2 minutes. Serve immediately.

MENTON SOUP

Yields 11 cups

3 tablespoons olive oil
2 medium-size onions, chopped
4 large cloves garlic, minced
6 cups Vegetable Stock (page 35)
4 large tomatoes or (28-ounce
   can) plum tomatoes, chopped
2 potatoes, cut into ½-inch cubes
2 medium-size zucchini, chopped
2 cups chopped green beans
2 cups cauliflower florets
1 cup cooked pinto or navy beans
¼ pound whole wheat spaghetti,
   broken into 1-inch pieces
¾ cup (6-ounce can) tomato paste
¾ cup chopped fresh parsley
2 tablespoons dried basil
1 tablespoon dried oregano
½ teaspoon pepper
   grated Parmesan cheese

Heat the olive oil in a Dutch oven; sauté the onion and 2 of the garlic cloves over medium heat until softened, about 5 minutes. Add the vegetable stock, tomatoes, potatoes, zucchini, green beans, and cauliflower. Bring to a boil. Stir in the pinto or navy beans; reduce heat to low. Simmer, uncovered, until vegetables are tender, about 25 minutes.

Stir in the spaghetti. Simmer, uncovered, until the spaghetti is tender, about 15 minutes.

In a small bowl, mix the tomato paste, parsley, basil, oregano, pepper, and remaining garlic; whisk into soup. Heat through.

Serve with Parmesan.

ZUCCHINI SOUP WITH
TOASTED CHEESE CUBES

6 to 8 servings

2 tablespoons butter
1 medium-size onion, chopped
5 cups Vegetable Stock (page 35)
6 medium-size zucchini, sliced
1 teaspoon dried basil
2 tablespoons lemon juice
3 tablespoons soy sauce
  white pepper, to taste
  Toasted Cheese Cubes (see
    following recipe)

Heat the butter in a Dutch oven or large saucepan; add the onion and sauté until softened. Add the vegetable stock, zucchini, and basil; cover and simmer 15 minutes, stirring occasionally. With a slotted spoon, remove 1 cup of the zucchini slices and set aside.

Transfer the remaining soup mixture in batches to a food processor or blender and process until smooth. Return to the pan; stir in the reserved zucchini slices. Add the lemon juice, soy sauce, and pepper. Reheat, or chill until ready to serve. Garnish with Toasted Cheese Cubes.

Toasted Cheese Cubes

Makes 2 cups cubes

¾ cup grated cheddar cheese
  (3 ounces)
1½ ounces cream cheese or kefir
  cheese
4 tablespoons butter
2 egg whites
4 slices whole wheat bread, cubed

Preheat oven to 400°F. Oil a baking sheet.

In a double boiler, melt the cheeses and butter. Remove from heat and add the egg whites, stirring until smooth.

In two batches, gently stir the bread cubes into the cheese mixture. Remove with a slotted spoon. If desired, at this point the cubes may be stored in the refrigerator for up to 2 days or in the freezer for up to a month.

Before serving, place the cubes on the baking sheet and bake until lightly toasted, about 8 minutes.

ORANGE-CARROT SOUP

6 to 8 servings

¼ cup butter
1 medium-size onion, chopped
4 cups Vegetable Stock (page 35)
4 to 5 medium-size carrots, cooked and drained
2 tablespoons whole wheat flour
6 ounces orange juice concentrate
¼ teaspoon pepper
1 tablespoon chopped dried chives
1 cup half-and-half
1 orange, thinly sliced

In a small skillet, melt 2 tablespoons butter; add onion and sauté until tender.

In a food processor or blender, place 2 cups vegetable stock, carrots, and sautéed onion; process until smooth.

In a large saucepan, melt the remaining butter; add the flour and cook until smooth and bubbly, stirring occasionally. Add the remaining stock and cook until slightly thick. Add the orange juice concentrate, pepper, chives, and carrot mixture; heat thoroughly. (If desired, soup may be stored up to 2 days at this point.)

Just before serving, heat the soup and add the half-and-half. Warm thoroughly but do not boil.

Ladle the soup into bowls and garnish each serving with an orange slice.

This soup is also good when served chilled.

SIDE DISHES

FRIED RICE AND TOFU

8 servings

4 tablespoons oil
2 eggs, beaten
½ pound firm tofu, drained and cubed
1 cup sliced mushrooms
1 stalk celery, chopped
½ cup alfalfa sprouts
2 scallions, chopped
4 cups cooked brown rice
1 cup peas
3 tablespoons soy sauce
  pinch of white pepper

In a wok or large skillet, heat 2 tablespoons oil until hot. Reduce heat to medium; add eggs and tofu. Stir lightly until eggs are almost set; remove from pan and set aside.

In the same pan, heat the remaining oil. Add the mushrooms, celery, sprouts, and scallions; stir-fry about 2 minutes. Add the rice; fry 3 to 5 minutes; continue stirring and add the peas and egg mixture. Gradually add the soy sauce and pepper.

Fried Rice and Tofu is tasty when served immediately or made in advance and reheated.

SAUTÉED CHERRY TOMATOES

6 servings

- 3 tablespoons butter
- 2 tablespoons honey
- ½ teaspoon dried oregano
- 3 scallions, sliced
- 4 cups cherry tomatoes
  freshly ground pepper, to taste
- ¼ cup chopped fresh parsley

Melt the butter in a large skillet over medium heat; add the honey and oregano and mix well. Increase the heat to high; add the scallions and tomatoes; cook until the tomatoes are warm, but not mushy, about 3 minutes. Remove from heat and season with pepper; stir in parsley. Serve immediately.

VEGETABLE TARTLETS WITH SESAME-SOY CRUST

Makes 8 tarts

- 1 Sesame-Soy Crust (see following recipe)
- 2 medium-size carrots, chopped
- 1 cup small cauliflower florets
- 1 cup peas
- 1 cup sliced mushrooms
- 2 tablespoons butter
- 2 tablespoons whole wheat flour
- 1 cup milk
- ⅔ cup (6-ounce can) tomato paste
- ½ teaspoon pepper
- ½ teaspoon dried marjoram
- 8 sprigs of parsley

Prepare Sesame-Soy Crust.
Preheat oven to 350°F.
Steam the carrots, cauliflower, peas, and mushrooms until crisp-tender. Spoon into the prepared Sesame-Soy Crusts, keeping the pastry in tart pans.
In a medium-size saucepan, melt the butter; add the flour and stir until bubbly. Gradually pour in the milk, continue cooking, and stir until the mixture is smooth and thick. Remove from heat; stir in the tomato paste, pepper, and marjoram.
Spoon enough tomato sauce over each tart to cover the vegetables. Bake for 20 minutes. Cool the tarts slightly; remove from pans. Garnish each with a sprig of parsley; serve immediately.

Sesame-Soy Crust

Makes 8 tart crusts or 1 piecrust

- ¾ cup whole wheat flour
- ¼ cup safflower oil
- 2 tablespoons sesame seeds
- 2 tablespoons soy flour
- 2 tablespoons wheat germ
- 2 tablespoons buttermilk

Preheat oven to 350°F. Lightly oil the bottoms of 8 tart pans, 4½ inches in diameter.
Combine all ingredients in a medium-size bowl. Toss with a fork until well mixed; press into the bottom and sides of the tart pans. (If desired, the crust may be used in a 9-inch pie plate.)
Prick the bottom of the crusts with a fork and bake for 10 minutes.

VEGETABLE EGG ROLLS WITH APRICOT SWEET-AND-SOUR SAUCE AND HOT MUSTARD SAUCE

Makes 20 rolls

3¼ cups safflower oil
2 cups finely shredded cabbage
1 cup alfalfa sprouts
1 stalk celery, finely chopped
1 carrot, finely grated
¼ cup finely chopped water chestnuts
¼ cup finely chopped bamboo shoots
¼ cup minced scallions
¼ cup finely chopped mushrooms
1 tablespoon soy sauce
½ teaspoon five-spice powder
10 egg roll skins
1 egg
Apricot Sweet-and-Sour Sauce (see accompanying recipe)
Hot Mustard Sauce (see accompanying recipe)

In a wok or large skillet, heat 4 tablespoons of the oil. Stir in cabbage, sprouts, celery, carrot, water chestnuts, bamboo shoots, scallions, and mushrooms. Stir-fry until vegetables are crisp-tender, about 2 minutes. Transfer vegetables to a colander and drain. Then stir in soy sauce and five-spice powder.

Cut each egg roll skin in half from corner to corner to form 2 triangles. Place a damp towel over the skins to keep them moist while assembling the egg rolls.

In a small bowl, beat the egg lightly. This will be used to seal the edges of the egg rolls.

To form the egg rolls: Place about 2 tablespoons of the vegetable filling at the flat base of the triangular egg roll skin. Fold the base up one turn to enclose the filling. Fold the side points in, one over the other. With your finger, seal these edges with the beaten egg; also moisten the triangle point with the egg. Continue rolling and press the edges in to a make a neat package.

After forming the egg rolls, cover them with a moist towel to prevent them from drying out.

In a wok or a large skillet, heat the remaining oil to 375°F. Deep fry the egg rolls until golden brown, 3 to 5 minutes. Remove from oil and drain on paper towels. Serve hot with Apricot Sweet-and-Sour Sauce and Hot Mustard Sauce.

These egg rolls are also tasty when prepared in advance and reheated in a 350°F oven for 10 to 15 minutes.

Apricot Sweet-and-Sour Sauce

Yields ½ cup

¼ cup water
3 tablespoons cider vinegar
2 tablespoons honey
8 dried apricot halves, chopped
1 teaspoon finely grated peeled
  ginger root
1 teaspoon minced scallion
1 teaspoon finely chopped green
  pepper

Place all ingredients in a food processor or blender; puree.

Pour the mixture into a small saucepan; bring to a boil, then simmer about 10 minutes. Cover and store in refrigerator.

Serve at room temperature with Vegetable Egg Rolls.

Hot Mustard Sauce

Yields ⅓ cup

¼ cup dry mustard
3½ tablespoons cold water

Combine the mustard and water; stir until smooth. Let stand 5 to 10 minutes before serving.

SESAME GREEN BEANS

6 servings

4 cups cut green beans
3 tablespoons soy sauce
1 tablespoon sesame oil
¼ teaspoon ground nutmeg
½ cup sesame seeds

Steam the green beans until crisp-tender, about 8 minutes.

Meanwhile, combine soy sauce, sesame oil, and nutmeg in a medium-size saucepan over low heat. Add the sesame seeds and stir until lightly browned. Add the steamed beans and toss lightly. Serve immediately.

BREADS

HERBED MUFFINS

Makes 14 muffins

2 cups whole wheat flour
2 teaspoons baking powder
2 tablespoons chopped fresh parsley
1 tablespoon dried basil
1 clove garlic, minced
1¼ cups milk
1 egg, beaten
3 tablespoons butter, melted
2 tablespoons honey

Preheat oven to 375°F. Generously oil enough cups in muffin tins for 14 muffins or line the cups with paper baking cups.

In a large bowl, mix flour, baking powder, parsley, basil, and garlic.

In a small bowl, combine the milk, egg, butter, and honey. Add to the dry ingredients, stirring just enough to moisten. Batter will be lumpy.

Spoon into muffin tins.

Bake until golden brown, about 25 minutes. Serve warm with Safflower Butter (page 30).

MANY-GRAIN MAPLE MUFFINS

Makes 18 muffins

¾ cup whole wheat flour
¾ cup yellow cornmeal
½ cup rye flour
2 teaspoons baking powder
½ cup rolled oats
1 egg
1½ cups milk
¼ cup safflower oil
¼ cup maple syrup

Preheat oven to 400°F. Oil enough cups in muffin tins for 18 muffins or line the cups with paper baking cups.

In a large bowl, combine the whole wheat flour, cornmeal, rye flour, and baking powder; stir in the oats.

In a medium-size bowl, beat the egg until light; add the milk, oil, and syrup. Add this mixture to the dry ingredients and stir until well combined.

Spoon the batter into muffin tins. Bake for 25 minutes. Serve warm with Apple Butter (page 29).

WHOLE WHEAT CRESCENT ROLLS

Makes 24 rolls

2 tablespoons dry yeast
1 cup warm water (110°F)
1 cup water
⅓ cup maple syrup
¾ cup safflower oil
3 cups whole wheat flour
3 cups whole wheat pastry flour

In a small bowl, dissolve the yeast in the warm water; stir in 1 teaspoon maple syrup; let sit for 5 minutes or until mixture is bubbly.

In a large bowl, mix the water, the remaining syrup, and oil. Add the yeast mixture; stir well. Add the whole wheat flour and whole wheat pastry flour; mix well. Cover the dough with plastic wrap and chill until the dough is firm, about 1 hour.

Preheat oven to 350°F. Oil 2 baking sheets.

Divide the dough in half. On a floured work surface, roll each half into a round shape, ½-inch thick. Cut each round into 12 pie-shaped wedges. Roll up each wedge starting from the large end; form into a crescent shape. Place rolls on the oiled baking sheets, cover lightly with plastic wrap, set in a warm place, and allow to rise about 30 minutes.

Bake 15 to 20 minutes. Serve warm with Safflower Butter (page 30).

DESERTS

CAROB CHIFFON PIE WITH HONEY-COCONUT CRUST

Makes 1 pie

Honey-Coconut Crust (see
   following recipe)
1 tablespoon unflavored gelatin
½ cup carob powder
½ cup water
¼ cup honey
4 eggs, separated
1 teaspoon vanilla extract

Prepare Honey-Coconut Crust.

Combine gelatin and carob in the top of a double boiler. Stir in the water and honey. Lightly beat egg yolks; add to carob mixture. Place over simmering water and cook, stirring constantly, until slightly thick, about 5 minutes. Stir in vanilla. Remove from heat and cool to room temperature.

Beat the egg whites until stiff; fold into cooled carob mixture, and pour into baked crust. Refrigerate 5 to 6 hours to set before serving.

If desired, garnish each serving with honey-sweetened whipped cream, chopped walnuts, or carob chips.

Honey-Coconut Crust

Makes 1 crust

1 cup wheat germ
⅓ cup unsweetened shredded
   coconut
3 tablespoons safflower oil
2 tablespoons honey

Preheat oven to 350°F.

In a medium-size bowl, combine all ingredients. Press into the bottom of a 9-inch pie plate.

Bake until lightly browned, about 10 minutes. Cool.

CAROB-PECAN TORTE

- ¾ cup butter
- 1¼ cups honey
- 3 eggs
- 3½ teaspoons vanilla extract
- ¾ cup carob powder
- 1 cup whole wheat flour
- 1½ teaspoons baking powder
- 1¾ cups finely chopped pecans
- 4 tablespoons milk
- 2 tablespoons butter, melted
- 2 cups heavy cream

Preheat oven to 350°F. Cut 9 pieces of waxed paper into 9-inch circles.

In a large bowl, cream the butter; add 1 cup of the honey. Beat in the eggs, one at a time. Then beat in 1½ teaspoons vanilla.

In a medium-size bowl, mix carob powder, flour, and baking powder. Add to the creamed mixture. Mix in 1½ cups pecans and the milk; stir until the nuts are evenly distributed.

Brush baking sheets with the melted butter. Place 1 to 2 waxed paper circles on baking sheets and brush each circle with butter. Place ½ cup of carob batter on each circle and with a spatula spread evenly to within 1 inch of the edges.

Bake until the center springs back when lightly touched, 10 to 12 minutes.

Remove the carob layers from the baking sheets and cool, still attached to the waxed paper, on a wire rack. Repeat with remaining batter.

Whip the heavy cream until stiff peaks form. Continue beating while adding the remaining honey and remaining vanilla.

To assemble the torte: Remove the waxed paper from one carob layer and place on a platter. Spread a layer of the whipped cream on top. Repeat layers, ending with a cake layer. Refrigerate the remaining whipped cream.

Cover the torte with plastic wrap and freeze at least 2 hours before serving. Remove from freezer and allow the torte to set at room temperature for 30 minutes before slicing.

Garnish the torte with the reserved whipped cream and sprinkle with the remaining pecans. Fresh sliced strawberries or other fruit also make an attractive and tasty garnish.

To serve, use a serrated knife to slice the torte into thin wedges.

FRENCH APPLE TART

1 cup unsalted butter
2 cups whole wheat flour
¼ cup toasted sesame seeds
¼ cup ground pecans or
    walnuts
1 teaspoon cider vinegar
1 egg, beaten
1 to 3 tablespoons orange juice, chilled
¼ cup dried apricots
1½ cups water
4 tablespoons honey
4 to 5 large baking apples

To make the crust: Cut ¾ cup of the butter into the flour by hand or in a food processor using the steel blade. Add sesame seeds, pecans or walnuts, vinegar, and egg; mix. Add 1 tablespoon of orange juice; mix in more juice if the mixture is too dry to form a ball. Turn mixture out onto work surface. Work with your hands just until the mixture forms a ball. Wrap the ball of crust in plastic wrap and chill for 1 hour. During this time prepare the glaze.

To make the glaze: Place the apricots and water in a 2-quart saucepan; bring to a boil. Cover, reduce heat, and simmer until apricots are soft, about 12 minutes. Puree mixture in a food processor or blender. Add 2 tablespoons of the honey. Bring glaze to room temperature. (Glaze will be thin.)

Preheat oven to 375°F. Roll out ½ of the dough between 2 sheets of waxed paper. Transfer the dough to a 10 or 11-inch French tart pan (preferably one with a removable bottom). Trim the edges of dough that extend beyond the pan. If the dough accidently tears, press it back together. (The remaining dough should be enough for an additional tart or piecrust. Refrigerate for several days, or freeze for up to 1 month.)

To make filling: Slice the apples ¼-inch thick. Arrange the slices in a circle on the crust; evenly overlap the edges. Melt the remaining butter with the remaining honey; pour over the apple slices.

Bake until the crust is firm and the apples are lightly browned on the edges, about 45 minutes. Cool; then, pour the apricot glaze over the tart; spread evenly. Serve slightly warm or at room temperature.

To make a larger tart, use a jelly-roll pan. Press a double crust in place and fill with twice as much apple filling, arranging apples in overlapping rows. Cover with a double recipe of apricot glaze. Cut into squares to serve.

HONEY-LEMON CHIFFON PIE WITH CAROB CHIP CRUMB CRUST

Makes 1 pie

1 Carob Chip Crumb Crust
   (see following recipe)
1 tablespoon unflavored gelatin
½ cup cold water
⅔ cup honey
½ cup lemon juice
1 teaspoon grated lemon rind
4 egg whites
½ cup heavy cream
   lemon slices

Prepare Carob Chip Crumb Crust. Set aside.

Soften gelatin in cold water in a small saucepan. Add ¼ cup of the honey, lemon juice, and lemon rind. Stir over low heat until the gelatin is completely dissolved. Transfer this mixture to a large bowl and refrigerate until the mixture reaches the consistency of egg whites. Beat until light.

In a separate bowl, beat the egg whites until stiff. Add ¼ cup honey and beat well. Fold the egg white mixture into the lemon-gelatin mixture.

Pour into the crust and chill 5 to 6 hours.

Before serving, beat the cream until soft peaks form; beat in the remaining honey.

Garnish each serving with the sweetened whipped cream and a lemon slice.

This pie is best when made the day it is to be served.

Carob Chip Crumb Crust

Makes 2 crusts

½ cup butter
¼ cup honey
2 eggs, beaten
¼ teaspoon vanilla extract
1 cup whole wheat flour
1 tablespoon nonfat dry milk
½ teaspoon baking soda
¼ cup chopped walnuts
½ cup carob chips

Preheat oven to 375°F. Oil 2 baking sheets.

In a large bowl, cream ¼ cup of the butter; add honey, eggs, and vanilla. Beat well. Stir in flour, dry milk, baking soda, walnuts, and carob chips. Drop the mixture by tablespoonfuls onto oiled baking sheets. Bake until browned, 10 to 15 minutes. Cool cookies on wire rack.

To make 1 crust: crumble 18 of the cookies in a food processor or blender. Melt the remaining butter and stir into the crumbs. Press the mixture into a 9-inch pie plate. Bake until the edges are lightly browned, about 8 minutes. Cool on wire rack.

Freeze the remaining cookies. When ready to use as a piecrust, thaw, crumble, and mix with ¼ cup melted butter.

PINEAPPLE-COCONUT SHERBET

2 cups (2 8-ounce cans) crushed
   pineapple
2 cups yogurt (page 24)
½ cup unsweetened shredded
   coconut
2 tablespoons honey

In a medium-size bowl, combine all ingredients and stir well. Pour into a shallow pan or freezer tray, and freeze until partially set. Transfer to a bowl, and beat 3 to 4 minutes. Pour into a container with cover and freeze until solid.

Soften at room temperature for about 15 minutes before serving.

RASPBERRY TRIFLE

6 servings

1 loaf Honey Spiced Pound Cake
   (see accompanying recipe)
½ cup orange juice
2 cups Raspberry Sauce (see
   accompanying recipe)
1 cup chopped pineapple
1 cup sliced almonds
3 cups Honey-Vanilla Creme
   Patisserie (see accompanying
   recipe)
½ cup heavy cream
1 tablespoon honey

Line the bottom of a 1½-quart trifle dish or glass soufflé dish with ½-inch-thick slices of the Honey-Spiced Pound Cake; trim the cake as necessary to fit the pan. Sprinkle with ¼ cup orange juice. Spread 1 cup of Raspberry Sauce over the cake and arrange ½ cup of the pineapple and ⅓ cup of the almonds on top of the sauce. Pour 1½ cups of the Honey-Vanilla Cream Patisserie over the layers and allow it to seep to the bottom of the dish.

Cut the remaining pound cake into cubes. Repeat layers, ending with the Creme Patisserie. Cover and refrigerate 6 to 8 hours before serving.

Just before serving, beat the heavy cream until it stands in soft peaks. Beat in the honey.

Garnish the trifle with the whipped cream and remaining almonds.

Honey-Spiced Pound Cake

Makes 2 cakes

3 cups whole wheat flour
2 teaspoons baking powder
1½ teaspoons baking soda
1 tablespoon ground cinnamon
½ teaspoon powdered ginger
¼ teaspoon ground cloves
¼ teaspoon ground allspice
¼ teaspoon ground nutmeg
2 eggs, beaten
1½ cups honey
½ cup safflower oil
½ cup orange juice
⅓ cup sour half-and-half or sour cream
1 cup coarsely chopped walnuts

Preheat oven to 325°F. Oil 2 loaf pans, 9 × 5-inches.

In a large bowl, mix the flour, baking powder, baking soda, cinnamon, ginger, cloves, allspice, and nutmeg.

In a separate bowl, combine the eggs, honey, oil, orange juice, and sour half-and-half or sour cream. Add to the flour mixture; stir until well blended. Stir in the walnuts.

Pour into the pans and bake for 45 to 55 minutes.

Raspberry Sauce

Yields about 2 cups

2 cups fresh raspberries or 2 10-ounce packages frozen unsweetened raspberries
3 tablespoons honey
1 teaspoon grated lemon rind
2 teaspoons cornstarch
¼ cup water

In a small saucepan, combine the raspberries, honey, and lemon rind. Stir over low heat until just below boiling. In a cup, combine the cornstarch and water; add to the raspberry mixture. Cook slowly until thick and smooth. Cover and chill in the refrigerator.

Use as a layer in Raspberry Trifle or as a cheesecake topping.

Honey-Vanilla Creme Patisserie

Yields about 3 cups

2 cups milk
6 egg yolks
½ cup honey
¼ cup whole wheat pastry flour
2 tablespoons butter
1 tablespoon vanilla extract
dash of ground nutmeg

In a 1-quart saucepan, bring milk to a boil.

Place yolks in another 1-quart saucepan; beat in honey, then flour. Add the boiling milk in a thin stream, stirring constantly. Simmer, stirring constantly, until the mixture thickens. Remove from heat; add butter and vanilla, beating until the butter melts. Sprinkle with nutmeg; cover, and chill.

WHOLE WHEAT PUFFS WITH ORANGE-HONEY ICE AND HOT CAROB SAUCE

Makes 8 large or 20 small puffs

¼ cup butter
½ cup boiling water
½ cup whole wheat pastry flour
2 eggs
  Orange-Honey Ice (see accompanying recipe)
  Hot Carob Sauce (see accompanying recipe)

Preheat oven to 400°F. Line a baking sheet with aluminum foil.

Place butter and water in a medium-size saucepan; bring to a rolling boil but do not let the water evaporate. Add the flour; stir vigorously. Cook, stirring constantly, until mixture forms a ball that does not separate; remove from heat and cool slightly. Add eggs, one at a time, beating vigorously after each addition, until the mixture is smooth.

Drop from a tablespoon, 2 inches apart, onto the baking sheet. Bake for 20 minutes; reduce heat to 350°F and continue baking until lightly browned, about 15 minutes. Remove puffs with a spatula; make a slit in the side of each to let steam escape. Cool on a wire rack.

To serve, slice the puffs into halves crosswise with a serrated knife. Fill each with a scoop of Orange-Honey Ice. Replace the tops; place in dessert bowls, and spoon Hot Carob Sauce over the top. Serve immediately.

If you want smaller puffs, drop the dough from a teaspoon onto the baking sheet and reduce each baking period by 5 minutes.

Because these puffs tend to absorb moisture, avoid making them on a humid day. Store unused puffs in a paper bag to preserve their original texture. If kept in plastic containers, they will become soggy.

Orange-Honey Ice

Yields about 1 quart

2 tablespoons unflavored gelatin
2 cups orange juice
1 cup heavy cream
¼ cup honey
1 teaspoon grated orange rind
½ teaspoon almond extract
½ cup finely chopped almonds

In a medium-size saucepan, combine the gelatin and orange juice; let stand 5 minutes to soften the gelatin. Then heat over low heat to dissolve the gelatin. Cool to room temperature.

Beat the cream until stiff; continue beating while adding the honey. Stir in the orange rind, almond extract, and almonds. Gently fold in the cooled gelatin mixture.

Spoon into a refrigerator tray, cover, and freeze until firm.

Hot Carob Sauce

Yields 2 cups

1 cup water
1 cup carob powder
⅔ cup maple syrup
2 eggs, beaten
4 tablespoons butter
2 teaspoons vanilla extract

In a medium-size saucepan, combine the water and carob powder until the powder is dissolved; bring to a boil, stirring constantly. Add the remaining ingredients and cook over low heat, stirring constantly, until thick and smooth.

The Hot Carob Sauce may be stored in the refrigerator and reheated to serve.

WHOLE WHEAT-ALMOND COOKIES

Makes about 72 cookies

1 cup butter, at room temperature
½ cup honey
1 egg, beaten
½ cup ground blanched almonds
1 teaspoon almond extract
2 cups whole wheat flour
1½ teaspoons baking powder
¾ cup blanched almond halves

Preheat oven to 350°F. Oil baking sheets.

In a large bowl, cream the butter; add the honey; beat in the egg. Stir in the ground almonds and almond extract; mix well.

In a separate bowl, mix the flour and baking powder. Gradually add to the butter mixture; mix well.

Shape the dough into 1-inch balls and place them about 2 inches apart on the baking sheet. Press an almond half on each ball and flatten the balls slightly.

Bake until golden brown, about 15 minutes. Repeat until all dough has been used.

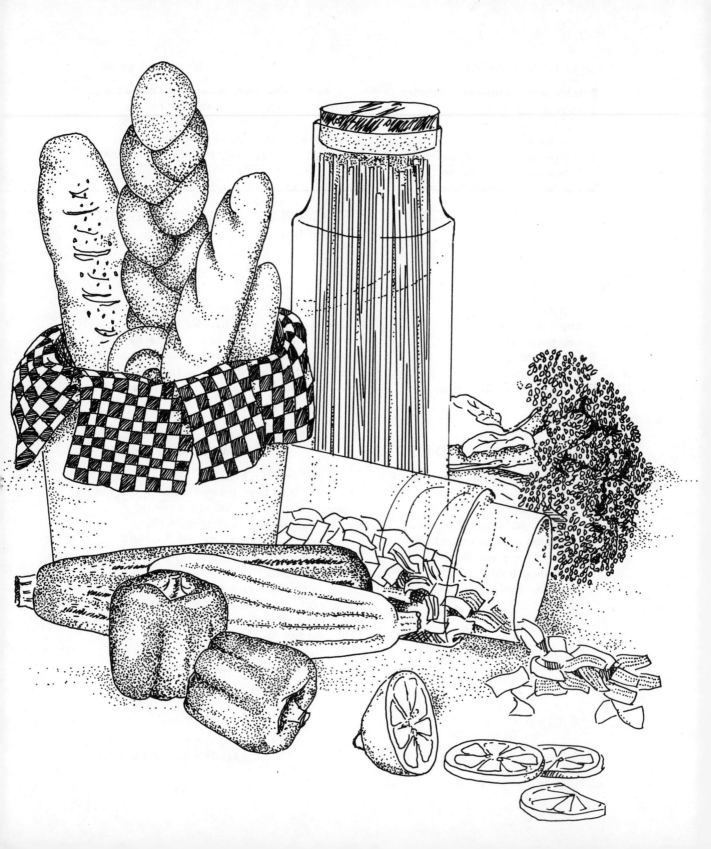

Holiday Feasts and Buffets

A buffet is an easy and attractive way to serve a large number of guests. In planning the buffet menus here, I had two main considerations: (1) foods that are easy to eat and (2) foods that do not suffer from standing. Also, the recipes I've chosen are easily augmented to accommodate a few more guests. If you desire, one or two dishes may be eliminated from the lengthy menus, with no harm done.

In arranging the buffet table, I put all items in a logical order. Plates, flatware, and napkins should be first. If an entree is to be served over rice, I put the rice before the entree. And, garnishes go next to the dish they accompany. As time for dessert approaches, I clear the buffet table and reset it with the dessert and an appropriate beverage.

These are very popular menus with holiday guests at my home; I'm sure your guests will enjoy them too. Bon appetit.

MENUS
HOLIDAY FEASTS AND BUFFETS

Ɣ Caponata
Cream of Mushroom Soup
Marinated Mixed Vegetables
Italian Carrot Salad
Vegetable Lasagna
Glazed Oranges

Ɣ Vegetable Terrine
Celery-Almond Soup
Marinated Herbed Tomatoes
Cranberry-Pineapple Sorbet
Nutloaf with Asparagus-Mushroom Sauce
Carrot-Honey Casserole
Lemon-Orange Mousse

Ɣ Spanish Green Salad with Lemon-Garlic Dressing
Whole Wheat French Bread
Vegetable Paella
Pumpkin Custard

𝒴 Eggplant Spread
Hummus
Harusame Salad with Soy Sauce Dressing
Calcutta Curry
Savory Tofu Rice
Sweet-and-Hot Chili Sauce
Curried Lentils
Mango Cream

𝒴 Roasted Pepper Appetizer
Escarole Soup
Cheese Sticks
Mixed Green Salad with Italian Dressing
Whole Wheat Spaghetti with Nutballs in Marinara Sauce
Zucchini Parmesan
Broccoli in Lemon Butter and Pine Nuts
Baked Pears with Lemon Cream

𝒴 Quesadillas with Guacamole
Vegetable-Cheese Nachos
Vegetable Enchiladas
Cheese Enchiladas
Refried Beans
Baked Chili Rellenos
Mexican Rice
Fiesta Salad

APPETIZERS AND BREADS

CAPONATA

6 to 8 servings

½ cup olive or safflower oil
1 medium-size onion, chopped
3 stalks celery, chopped
2 cloves garlic, minced
1 medium-size eggplant, peeled and
    cut into ½-inch cubes
6 medium-size tomatoes, cut into
    ½-inch cubes
2 tablespoons cider vinegar
2 tablespoons tomato paste
1 tablespoon chopped fresh parsley
1 teaspoon dried basil
½ teaspoon pepper

In a large skillet, heat the oil and sauté the onion, celery, and garlic until tender. Add the remaining ingredients; stir well to combine. Continue to cook, uncovered, until the vegetables are tender, about 15 minutes.

Chill and serve cold as an appetizer with crusty bread or thin toast triangles.

Caponata will keep about 1 week in the refrigerator.

CHEESE STICKS

Makes 3 dozen

1 cup whole wheat pastry flour
¼ teaspoon pepper
¼ cup butter
⅓ cup grated sharp cheddar cheese
    (1 ounce)
2 tablespoons grated Parmesan
    cheese
1 tablespoon ice water

Preheat oven to 350°F.

In a medium-size bowl, mix flour and pepper. With a pastry blender, cut in the butter until mixture resembles crumbs. Blend in the cheeses; add ice water. Stir with a fork until mixture forms a ball.

Place the ball on a lightly floured work surface. With a rolling pin, roll out until approximately ¼-inch thick. Cut into 3 × ½-inch sticks.

Bake on ungreased baking sheets until lightly browned, 10 minutes. Serve warm or at room temperature.

These sticks can be made ahead, covered, and refrigerated until ready to bake.

EGGPLANT SPREAD

1 medium-size eggplant
2 scallions, minced
2 teaspoons safflower oil
2 teaspoons tomato paste
2 cloves garlic, minced
2 teaspoons lemon juice
½ teaspoon pepper
  dash of ground cumin

Yields about 1 cup

Preheat oven to 350°F.

With a fork, pierce eggplant skin in several places; place on oven rack and bake until tender, 40 to 50 minutes. Cool slightly; split the eggplant, and scoop the inside into a medium-size bowl. Mash well. Stir in the remaining ingredients; cover and chill.

Serve as an appetizer spread on cucumber slices or whole wheat crackers.

HUMMUS

2 tablespoons safflower oil
¼ cup chopped onion
½ cup minced fresh parsley
2 cloves garlic, minced
1 teaspoon dried basil
½ teaspoon ground coriander
½ teaspoon dried oregano
¼ teaspoon pepper
  dash of ground cumin
3 cups cooked chick-peas
4 tablespoons lemon juice
¼ cup toasted sesame seeds

Yields about 3½ cups

Heat oil in a small skillet; sauté onion until soft. Add parsley, garlic, basil, coriander, oregano, pepper, and cumin. Stir over medium heat just long enough to soften the parsley.

In a food processor or blender, combine the chick-peas and lemon juice; process until smooth. Stir into onion-and-herb mixture; add sesame seeds. Refrigerate.

Use Hummus as a dip with whole wheat crackers or as a spread on small open-faced appetizers made with whole wheat bread or cucumber slices and garnished with tomato slices. Or, make sandwiches with pita bread. Stuff pita bread pockets with the Hummus, shredded lettuce, chopped tomatoes, shredded cheese, and sprouts.

QUESADILLAS WITH GUACAMOLE

6 to 8 servings

4 **flour tortillas**
safflower oil
1 **cup grated cheddar cheese (4 ounces)**
½ **cup diced tomatoes**
⅓ **cup chopped green chilies**
4 **teaspoons chopped scallions**
1 **cup Guacamole (see following recipe)**

Pour ¼ inch of oil in a large skillet; heat. One at a time, fry the tortillas on both sides until light brown, puffy, and crisp. Drain on paper towels. (This step may be done a day or two in advance.)

Near serving time, sprinkle each tortilla with ¼ cup cheese and top with 2 tablespoons tomatoes, 2 teaspoons chilies, and 1 teaspoon scallions. Place on a broiler rack 4 to 6 inches from heat until cheese has melted, about 4 minutes.

Spoon about ¼ cup of Guacamole into the center. To serve, cut each tortilla into 4 to 6 wedges.

Guacamole

Yields about 2 cups

2 **avocados**
1 **medium-size tomato, finely chopped**
¼ **cup minced onion**
2 **green chilies, minced**
1 **tablespoon lemon juice**
1 **clove garlic, minced**
½ **teaspoon pepper**
dash of hot pepper sauce

Mash the avocados until very smooth, or a little chunky, if desired. Stir in the remaining ingredients. Cover and refrigerate at least 1 hour before serving.

Serve as a topping on Quesadillas, as a dip for corn chips, or as a side dish.

ROASTED PEPPER APPETIZER

6 servings

    6 green, yellow, or red peppers
    ⅓ cup lemon juice
    ½ cup olive or safflower oil

Place peppers on a broiler pan close to the heating element; broil, turning often, until they are charred. Or, spear each of the peppers on skewers and char them one at a time over a medium-high gas flame, turning frequently to char evenly. The outer skin should be entirely blackened and blistered.

Using a colander, hold the charred peppers under a stream of cool water until they are cool enough to handle. Peel off the blackened skins, and cut into ½-inch strips.

In a large bowl, combine the lemon juice and oil. Stir in the pepper strips. Let stand at room temperature for 1 hour, stirring occasionally. Using a slotted spoon, remove peppers from marinade and serve. Or, if desired, refrigerate, covered, for 2 to 3 hours before serving.

VEGETABLE-CHEESE NACHOS

6 servings

    3 medium-size zucchinis, cut into
          ¼-inch slices
    4 tablespoons chopped green chilies
    2 cups grated Monterey Jack cheese
          (8 ounces)
       Tomato Hot Sauce (page 34)

Arrange the zucchini slices in overlapping rows on an ovenproof platter. Top evenly with the chilies and grated cheese.

Place on boiler rack 4 to 6 inches from heat until cheese has melted, about 5 minutes.

Serve with a bowl of Tomato Hot Sauce for dipping.

VEGETABLE TERRINE

2¼ cups Vegetable Stock (page 35)
3 tablespoons unflavored gelatin
¼ teaspoon white pepper
10 to 12 spears asparagus, steamed and
cooled
2 medium-size carrots, shredded
2 cups peas, cooked and cooled
2 cups cut wax beans, steamed and
cooled
1 cup chopped spinach, cooked,
drained, and cooled
6 cooked artichoke hearts, drained
and halved
1 cup yogurt (page 24)
½ cup Mayonnaise (page 31)
2 teaspoons Mustard (page 31)
1 teaspoon lemon juice
½ teaspoon garlic powder
¼ teaspoon paprika

Chill a 1½-quart soufflé dish in the freezer.

Pour the vegetable stock into a large saucepan. Add the gelatin and let stand 5 minutes to soften. Place over low heat, stirring until gelatin is dissolved. Remove from heat; season with pepper. Cool to room temperature.

Remove the soufflé dish from the freezer and quickly swirl several tablespoons of the gelatin mixture around the bottom. It should set almost immediately.

Crisscross the asparagus spears over the gelatin on the bottom of the mold to make a lattice pattern.

Layer the carrots over the asparagus spears. Layer the remaining vegetables in this order: peas, wax beans, and spinach. Press the artichoke hearts into the spinach layer in a circular arrangement with 1 in the center.

Slowly pour on the remaining gelatin mixture, allowing it to seep through the layers. Refrigerate until set, 3 to 4 hours.

In a food processor or blender, process the yogurt, mayonnaise, mustard, lemon juice, garlic, and paprika until smooth. Chill.

To serve, loosen the edges of the mold with a knife. Dip the bottom of the mold briefly in hot water; invert it onto a round platter. Cut into wedges with a serrated knife and top each with a serving of the yogurt sauce.

WHOLE WHEAT FRENCH BREAD

Makes 2 loaves

2½ to 3 cups whole wheat pastry flour
   2 tablespoons dry yeast
   2 teaspoons honey
   2 cups warm water (115°F)
   3 cups whole wheat flour
      cornmeal, for dusting baking
       sheet

In a large bowl, combine 2½ cups whole wheat pastry flour and yeast; mix well. In a medium-size bowl, mix honey and water; add to the flour mixture. Let stand for 5 minutes.

Add the remaining pastry flour and the whole wheat flour, 1 cup at a time. Knead about 10 minutes. Place in a large bowl, cover with plastic wrap, and let rise in a warm place until doubled in bulk, about 1 hour.

Lightly oil a baking sheet and dust with cornmeal.

Punch down the dough and divide in half. With a rolling pin, shape each half into a 10 × 14-inch rectangle. With the long side toward you, roll tightly; pinch the ends and turn under. Place on the prepared baking sheet, seam side down. With a knife, make 5 diagonal slices on the top of each loaf.

Place the baking sheet on a rack in the middle of a cold oven. Set a pan of hot water underneath; let rise until doubled in bulk, 20 to 30 minutes. Remove the pan of water and the baking sheet from the oven. Set the oven temperature at 425°F. Brush the top of each loaf with cold water. Place in the partially heated oven and bake until lightly browned and crusty, 20 to 25 minutes.

Serve warm with Herb Butter (page 30).

MAIN COURSES

CALCUTTA CURRY

4 to 6 servings

¼ cup safflower oil or butter
2 cups sliced mushrooms
2 carrots, diced
1 medium-size onion, chopped
¼ cup chopped celery
1 to 2 tablespoons curry powder
½ teaspoon pepper
¼ teaspoon powdered ginger
¼ teaspoon ground cumin
1½ cups half-and-half
¼ cup Vegetable Stock (page 35)
2 tablespoons apple juice
2 tablespoons cornstarch
¼ cup water
2 cups peas, cooked
Savory Tofu Rice (see
    accompanying recipe)

In a Dutch oven or large saucepan, heat the oil or butter; sauté the mushrooms, carrots, onion, celery, and curry powder until onion is tender. Stir in the pepper, ginger, cumin, half-and-half, stock, and apple juice; simmer for 5 minutes, stirring occasionally.

Combine the cornstarch and water; mix well. Stir into the curry mixture; cook over medium heat, stirring constantly until thick, about 5 minutes. Stir in the peas; heat through.

Serve hot over Savory Tofu Rice and present two or more of these condiments: raisins, peanuts, shredded unsweetened coconut, pineapple chunks, Sweet-and-Hot Chili Sauce (see accompanying recipe).

Savory Tofu Rice

6 servings

6 whole cloves
3 peppercorns
1½ cups uncooked brown rice
¼ teaspoon tumeric
2½ cups water
5 tablespoons safflower oil
½ pound firm tofu, drained and cut
    into 1-inch cubes
2 scallions, chopped
1 clove garlic, minced
1 medium-size carrot, chopped
½ medium-size green pepper,
    chopped
1 cup raw cashews
½ cup raisins
2 eggs, beaten
2 tablespoons soy sauce

Tie the whole cloves and peppercorns in a cheesecloth bag; place the bag in a large saucepan. Add rice, tumeric, and water. Cover pan and bring to a boil over high heat; reduce heat to low and simmer, covered, until rice is tender and liquid is absorbed, 20 to 30 minutes.

While the rice is cooking, heat 2 tablespoons of the oil in a large skillet. Spoon in the tofu and stir-fry gently until lightly browned. Remove from pan and set aside.

In the skillet, heat 2 tablespoons oil. Add the scallions, garlic, carrot, and green pepper; cook, stirring occasionally until the vegetables are crisp-tender, 5 minutes. Add the cashews and raisins; cook for an additional 3 minutes. Remove from pan and set aside.

Heat the remaining oil in the skillet; add the eggs and scramble; remove from pan while still moist.

When the rice is cooked, remove the bag of spices. Stir in the vegetables, eggs, and soy sauce; gently toss in the fried tofu. Heat through.

Sweet-and-Hot Chili Sauce

Yields 1¼ cups

1 cup cider vinegar
½ cup honey
½ cup golden raisins
2 cloves garlic, minced
1 teaspoon powdered ginger
½ teaspoon red pepper flakes

In a medium-size saucepan, combine all ingredients; bring to a boil over high heat. Reduce heat and simmer until raisins are soft, about 45 minutes. Remove from heat and cool.

In a food processor or blender, process until smooth. Cover and refrigerate. Bring to room temperature to serve.

CHEESE ENCHILADAS

1 tablespoon safflower oil
1 medium-size onion, chopped
1½ cups (15-ounce can) tomato puree
¼ cup tomato sauce
1 clove garlic, minced
1 teaspoon chili powder
¼ teaspoon ground cumin
¼ teaspoon dried oregano
2 drops hot pepper sauce
   pinch of cayenne pepper
¾ cup shredded Monterey Jack
   cheese (3 ounces)
1 cup shredded cheddar cheese
   (4 ounces)
1 scallion, minced
1 tablespoon chopped fresh parsley
6 soft corn tortillas
1 cup yogurt (page 24)

In a large skillet, heat oil; add onion, and sauté until soft. Stir in the tomato puree, tomato sauce, garlic, chili powder, cumin, oregano, pepper sauce, and cayenne. Cover and simmer for 20 minutes; set aside.

In a medium-size bowl, mix the Monterey Jack, ½ cup of the cheddar cheese, the scallion, and parsley; set aside.

Heat ¼ inch oil in a large skillet. With tongs, dip each tortilla into the tomato mixture, then place in the skillet. Fry a very short time to soften the tortilla; do not allow the edges to become crisp. Remove from the oil and drain on paper towels; repeat with remaining tortillas.

Preheat oven to 350°F. Oil a 6 × 10-inch baking dish.

Assemble the enchiladas by placing 2 heaping tablespoons of the cheese mixture in each tortilla; roll. Place side by side, seam side down, in the prepared dish. Pour on the remaining sauce. Sprinkle on the remaining ½ cup cheddar cheese. (If desired, the enchiladas may be refrigerated for up to 2 days at this point. Before baking, bring to room temperature.) Bake about 20 minutes.

Serve yogurt as a garnish for each serving.

NUTLOAF WITH ASPARAGUS-MUSHROOM SAUCE

2 tablespoons butter
3 stalks celery, chopped
1 medium-size onion, minced
2 tablespoons chopped fresh parsley
1 cup chopped toasted unsalted
  cashews
½ cup chopped walnuts
½ cup almonds or pecans, ground
  into flour
½ cup wheat germ
¼ cup rolled oats
¼ cup sunflower seeds
2 tablespoons soy flour
1 cup cottage cheese
½ cup cooked brown rice
3 eggs, beaten
3 tablespoons tomato paste
1 tablespoon soy sauce
½ teaspoon paprika
¼ teaspoon pepper
  Asparagus-Mushroom Sauce
    (see following recipe)

Preheat oven to 400°F. Oil a 9 × 5-inch loaf pan.

In a large skillet, melt the butter; sauté the celery and onion. Transfer to a large bowl and combine with the remaining ingredients except the Asparagus-Mushroom Sauce. Spoon into the loaf pan.

Bake for 50 to 60 minutes.

To serve, slice and top each serving with Asparagus-Mushroom Sauce.

Asparagus-Mushroom Sauce

4 tablespoons butter
¾ pound mushrooms, sliced
¼ cup chopped onion
2 cloves garlic, minced
4 tablespoons whole wheat flour
2½ cups milk
½ pound asparagus, chopped and
  steamed
2 tablespoons soy sauce
1 teaspoon dried tarragon
¼ teaspoon white pepper

In a medium-size saucepan, melt the butter. Stir in the mushrooms, onion, and garlic; sauté until tender. Stir in the flour; whisk in the milk; stir constantly until the mixture is smooth. Cook, stirring, until the sauce thickens. Then stir in the remaining ingredients; heat through.

VEGETABLE ENCHILADAS

6 servings

1 cup tomatoes, pureed
¼ cup finely chopped green chilies
¼ cup finely chopped onion
¼ cup heavy cream
1 egg, beaten
1 teaspoon chili powder
2 drops hot pepper sauce
2 tablespoons safflower oil
1 cup coarsely grated zucchini
1 cup sliced mushrooms
1 cup green beans, cut into ¼-inch pieces
½ cup finely chopped green pepper
¼ cup finely chopped celery
1 clove garlic, minced
   dash of chili powder
   dash of ground cumin
   dash of pepper
6 soft corn tortillas

In a medium-size bowl, mix tomatoes, chilies, onion, cream, egg, chili powder, and pepper sauce. Set aside.

In a large skillet, heat the oil; add the zucchini, mushrooms, green beans, green pepper, celery, and garlic. Cover and cook, stirring occasionally, until the vegetables are tender. Stir in the additional chili powder, the cumin, and pepper. Set aside.

Heat ¼ inch oil in a large skillet. With tongs, dip each tortilla into the tomato sauce mixture, then place in the skillet. Fry a very short time to soften the tortilla; do not allow the edges to become crisp. Remove from the oil and drain on paper towels. Repeat with remaining tortillas.

Preheat oven to 350°F. Oil a 6 × 10-inch baking dish.

Assemble the enchiladas by placing 3 heaping tablespoons of the vegetable filling in each tortilla; roll. Place in the baking dish, seam side down. Pour on the remaining sauce. (If desired, the enchilada may be refrigerated for up to 2 days at this point. Before baking, bring to room temperature.) Bake in the preheated oven about 20 minutes.

VEGETABLE PAELLA

¼ cup olive oil
2 stalks celery, sliced ¼-inch thick
2 small zucchini, sliced ¼-inch thick
1 medium-size green pepper,
    chopped into ½-inch cubes
1 medium-size red pepper, chopped
    into ½-inch cubes
1 medium-size onion, chopped
2 cloves garlic, minced
3 cups (28-ounce can) tomatoes,
    into quarters
1 cup raw cashews
1 teaspoon dried thyme
½ teaspoon ground cumin
½ teaspoon dried oregano
½ teaspoon cayenne pepper
2¾ cups Vegetable Stock (page 35)
2 cups uncooked brown rice
2 cups raw wheat berries
1 tablespoon lemon juice
1 teaspoon safflower oil
¾ pound broccoli, chopped and
    steamed
1 cup peas, cooked
½ cup corn, cooked
⅔ cup grated Parmesan cheese
    (5 ounces)
4 tablespoons tomato paste
8 to 10 eggs
    freshly ground pepper

In a Dutch oven, heat olive oil. Add celery, zucchini, green pepper, red pepper, onion, and garlic. Cook until onion is tender. Stir in tomatoes, cashews, thyme, cumin, oregano, cayenne, vegetable stock, rice, wheat berries, and lemon juice. Mix well and bring to a boil. Reduce heat and simmer 45 minutes, stirring occasionally.

After 30 minutes, preheat oven to 350°F. Lightly oil a 12-inch paella pan or a shallow baking dish.

Stir in broccoli, peas, corn, Parmesan, and tomato paste. (If desired, the dish may be stored in the refrigerator for a day at this point. If it has been stored, heat the mixture before proceeding with the recipe directions.) Spoon the mixture into the baking pan. With the back of a spoon, make a depression in the mixture for each of the eggs. Carefully break an egg into each of the depressions. Sprinkle each egg wth pepper. Bake, covered, until eggs are set, 15 to 18 minutes.

WHOLE WHEAT SPAGHETTI WITH NUTBALLS IN MARINARA SAUCE

6 servings

Marinara Sauce (see
  accompanying recipe)
Nutballs (see accompanying
  recipe)
8 ounces whole wheat spaghetti
Parmesan cheese, freshly grated

One day in advance of serving, prepare the Marinara Sauce and refrigerate.

Prepare the Nutballs. Heat the Marinara Sauce; gently stir in the Nutballs, heat through.

Fill a Dutch oven or deep pot with water; bring water to a full boil. Keep the water at a steady boil as you slowly lower in the pasta. Reduce heat; cover and cook, stirring occasionally until tender, 10 to 15 minutes. Drain.

Serve the spaghetti topped with Nutballs in Marinara Sauce and the Parmesan cheese.

Marinara Sauce

Yields 4 cups

1 tablespoon safflower oil
1 tablespoon olive oil
1 tablespoon butter
1 small onion, chopped
2 cloves garlic, minced
½ pound mushrooms, sliced
1 medium-size carrot, grated
1 stalk celery, finely chopped
2 tablespoons finely chopped green
  pepper
2 tablespoons chopped fresh parsley
1 bay leaf
1 teaspoon dried oregano
½ teaspoon dried thyme
¼ teaspoon dried basil
¼ teaspoon pepper
3 cups (28-ounce can) tomatoes, cut
  into quarters
⅔ cup (6-ounce can) tomato paste
  cayenne pepper, to taste

In a large saucepan, heat the safflower oil, olive oil, and butter. Stir in the onion, garlic, and mushrooms; sauté until softened. Add the carrot, celery, green pepper, parsley, bay leaf, oregano, thyme, basil, and pepper. Stir well; add the tomatoes and tomato paste. Add cayenne pepper. Cover, reduce heat, and simmer for 30 minutes. Remove the bay leaf.

This sauce becomes tastier with time. If possible, make a day or two in advance of serving and refrigerate until ready to use.

Nutballs

1 cup whole wheat bread crumbs or
   whole wheat cracker crumbs
¾ cup grated cheddar cheese
   (3 ounces)
¾ cup finely chopped pecans
2 eggs, beaten
1 small onion, minced
1 clove garlic, minced
1 tablespoon chopped fresh parsley
1 teaspoon soy sauce
½ teaspoon ground sage
¼ teaspoon pepper

Preheat oven to 350°F. Lightly oil a baking sheet.

In a large bowl, combine all of the ingredients; stir well. Form the mixture into about 36 balls the size of walnuts.

Place the balls on the baking sheet. Bake until lightly browned, about 15 minutes. If you prefer, the balls may be browned in oil in a skillet.

VEGETABLE LASAGNA

10 whole wheat lasagna noodles
   (8 ounces)
2 tablespoons olive oil
2 pounds spinach
½ pound mushrooms, sliced
2 medium-size carrots, grated
1 medium-size onion, chopped
2 cloves garlic, minced
1½ cups (15-ounce jar) tomato sauce
1¼ cups (12-ounce can) tomato paste
1½ teaspoons dried oregano
1 teaspoon dried basil
3 cups ricotta cheese
2 eggs
4 cups grated Monterey Jack cheese
   (16 ounces), or 2 cups grated
   mozzarella cheese (8 ounces)
   and 2 cups grated Monterey
   Jack cheese (8 ounces)
1 cup freshly grated Parmesan
   cheese (4 ounces)

Fill a large saucepan with water. Bring water to a full boil. Add lasagna noodles, reduce heat, and cook noodles in simmering water until tender, about 7 minutes; drain. Mix 2 teaspoons oil with noodles and set aside.

Rinse spinach well. In a medium-size saucepan, cook spinach, covered, without water except for the drops that cling to the leaves. Reduce heat when steam forms, and cook 3 to 5 minutes. Drain and chop.

Preheat oven to 375°F. Oil a 13 × 9-inch ovenproof casserole.

In a large saucepan, heat the remaining oil; cook mushrooms, carrots, onion, and garlic until tender but not brown. Stir in tomato sauce, tomato paste, oregano, and basil.

In a small bowl, beat eggs into ricotta cheese until smooth. In the casserole, place a layer of ½ of the noodles; then ½ of the ricotta cheese mixture, spinach, Monterey Jack cheese, and sauce; repeat layers.

Bake for 30 to 40 minutes. Sprinkle with about ½ cup of the Parmesan cheese. Let stand about 10 minutes before slicing. Serve with the remaining Parmesan cheese.

SALADS

FIESTA SALAD

6 servings

2 cups cubed jicama
1 small cucumber, cubed
1 orange, cubed
2 tablespoons lemon juice
1 tablespoon grated lemon rind
dash of ground cinnamon
romaine lettuce

In a large bowl, toss the jicama, cucumber, and orange. Add the lemon juice, lemon rind, and cinnamon; toss to coat. Cover and chill.
Serve on beds of lettuce.

HARUSAME *SALAD WITH SOY SAUCE DRESSING*

6 servings

1½ cups *Harusame* noodles
1 tablespoon safflower oil
2 eggs, scrambled and cut into strips
1 cucumber, cut into julienne strips
1 large tomato, cut into wedges
2 scallions, sliced
1 large stalk celery, cut into julienne strips
¼ pound mushrooms, sliced
¼ pound pea pods, blanched and cooled
1 cup bean sprouts
1 medium-size zucchini, cut into julienne strips
1 medium-size red or green pepper, cut into julienne strips
Soy Sauce Dressing (see following recipe)

Place the *Harusame* noodles in a large bowl; pour on enough boiling water to cover them; add oil and let stand until soft, 5 to 12 minutes. Rinse with cold water, drain, and chill. With kitchen shears, cut into shorter strands. Spread evenly on the bottom of a serving platter.

Arrange the remaining ingredients, except the dressing, attractively in clumps over the noodles.

Pour Soy Sauce Dressing over the entire salad just before serving.

Other vegetables are also tasty in this salad.

Soy Sauce Dressing

Yields ⅔ cup

6 tablespoons cider vinegar
6 tablespoons soy sauce
2 tablespoons honey
2 teaspoons sesame oil

Combine all ingredients. Serve on *Harusame* Salad.

ITALIAN CARROT SALAD

6 medium-size carrots, cut into
  julienne strips
2 stalks celery, cut into julienne
  strips
4 tablespoons olive oil
2 tablespoons lemon juice
1 teaspoon honey
½ teaspoon freshly ground pepper

In a medium-size bowl, toss carrot and celery strips; dress with olive oil and toss lightly.

In a cup, combine lemon juice, honey, and pepper. Add to salad and toss well. Chill about 1 hour before serving.

MIXED GREEN SALAD WITH ITALIAN DRESSING

6 servings

¼ head romaine lettuce, torn
½ head curly endive, torn
1 small head red-leaf lettuce, torn
½ cucumber, thinly sliced
¼ red onion, cut into slivers
½ cup chick-peas
  Italian Dressing (see following
  recipe)

In a large bowl, toss the romaine, endive, red-leaf lettuce, cucumber, onion, and chick-peas. Just before serving, toss again with Italian Dressing.

Italian Dressing

Yields 1 cup

½ cup cider vinegar
¼ cup olive or safflower oil
1 teaspoon minced onion
½ teaspoon minced fresh parsley
½ teaspoon minced fresh chives
½ teaspoon dried oregano
¼ teaspoon dry mustard
⅛ teaspoon garlic powder
  dash of white pepper
  dash of cayenne pepper

Combine all ingredients and mix well. Refrigerate at least 1 hour.

SPANISH GREEN SALAD WITH LEMON-GARLIC DRESSING

8 to 10 servings

3 quarts mixed salad greens, torn into bite-size pieces and chilled
1 large onion, thinly sliced and separated into rings
4 oranges, peeled and sliced
Lemon-Garlic Dressing (see following recipe)

In a large salad bowl, toss salad greens, onion, and oranges. Remove garlic from the Lemon-Garlic Dressing and pour over the salad. Toss again. Serve immediately.

Lemon-Garlic Dressing

Yields 1 cup

½ cup olive oil
¼ cup lemon juice
½ teaspoon freshly ground pepper
2 cloves garlic, peeled, halved, and speared on toothpicks

In a small bowl, combine oil, lemon juice, and pepper. Drop in the garlic spears. Let stand at room temperature about 1 hour. Remove garlic immediately prior to serving.

SOUPS

CELERY-ALMOND SOUP

6 servings

6 tablespoons butter
10 stalks celery, chopped
1 tablespoon curry powder
3 cups Vegetable Stock (page 35)
2 tablespoons chopped fresh parsley
3 cups milk or half-and-half
¼ teaspoon pepper
¼ cup heavy cream
2 tablespoons slivered almonds

In a medium-size saucepan, melt butter over low heat. Add celery and curry powder; cook about 10 minutes, stirring occasionally. Stir in the vegetable stock and parsley. Bring mixture to a boil; then reduce heat, cover, and simmer 20 minutes. Stir in milk and pepper.

Transfer mixture to a food processor or blender. Process until almost smooth; small bits of celery should remain for texture.

Return pureed soup to the saucepan and warm through. Stir in the heavy cream and almonds just before serving.

CREAM OF MUSHROOM SOUP

6 to 8 servings

1 pound mushrooms
6 tablespoons butter
1 small onion, minced
3 tablespoons whole wheat flour
6 cups Vegetable Stock (page 35)
2 tablespoons soy sauce
  white pepper, to taste
1 tablespoon lemon juice
⅓ cup slivered almonds
2 egg yolks
¾ cup half-and-half
3 tablespoons minced fresh parsley

Remove stems from mushrooms; chop stems finely and set aside. Slice mushroom caps and set aside.

In a Dutch oven or large saucepan, melt 4 tablespoons butter, add onions, and cook slowly until tender but not brown. Stir in flour and cook over medium heat, stirring constantly, for 2 to 3 minutes. Remove from heat and pour in the stock. Add soy sauce and pepper. Stir in mushroom stems; cover and simmer gently for 20 to 25 minutes. Strain; return to pot.

Add sliced mushroom caps and lemon juice, cover, and cook 10 minutes. Stir in almonds. (If desired at this point, the soup may be stored for a day. If soup has been stored, reheat in a covered saucepan to just a simmer before continuing recipe.)

Beat egg yolks and half-and-half; gradually add some of the hot soup. Return mixture to soup in pan. Heat for 2 minutes, but do not boil.

Garnish each serving with parsley.

ESCAROLE SOUP

6 servings

3 tablespoons butter
1 large onion, chopped
2 carrots, diced
1 stalk celery, diced
1 head escarole, shredded
5 cups Vegetable Stock (page 35)
¼ cup uncooked brown rice
2 tablespoons soy sauce
½ teaspoon pepper
¼ teaspoon dried thyme leaves
6 tablespoons sliced almonds
  Parmesan cheese, freshly grated

In Dutch oven or large saucepan, melt the butter and sauté the onion until tender but not browned. Add the carrots and celery; cook 3 minutes, stirring occasionally. Add the escarole and cook, stirring, for 2 minutes. Stir in the stock, rice, soy sauce, pepper, and thyme. Bring to a boil, reduce heat, cover, and simmer until rice is tender, 30 to 40 minutes.

Garnish each serving with 1 tablespoon sliced almonds. Serve with Parmesan cheese.

SIDE DISHES

BAKED CHILI RELLENOS

6 servings

6 fresh green chilies or 2 3-ounce
  cans green chilies, seeded
¼ cup chopped scallions
2 cups grated Monterey Jack cheese
  (8 ounces)
6 eggs, separated
2 tablespoons butter, melted
½ teaspoon ground cumin
½ teaspoon pepper
  Tomato Hot Sauce (page 34), at
  room temperature

Preheat oven to 350°F. Butter a 1½-quart soufflé dish.

Roast and peel fresh chilies. Layer ½ of the chilies, scallions, and cheese in the bottom of the soufflé dish. Repeat layers.

In a large bowl, beat the egg whites until soft peaks form. In a small bowl, lightly beat the yolks. Fold the yolks into the beaten whites; then fold in the remaining ingredients. Pour this mixture into the soufflé dish.

Bake until the top is puffed and lightly browned, 35 to 40 minutes. Serve immediately with the Tomato Hot Sauce.

BROCCOLI IN LEMON BUTTER AND PINE NUTS

6 servings

3 tablespoons butter
3 tablespoons pine nuts
2 tablespoons lemon juice
  freshly ground pepper, to taste
2 pounds broccoli stalks, steamed
  and kept warm

About 10 minutes before serving, melt the butter in a small skillet over medium heat. Add the pine nuts and cook 3 minutes, stirring constantly. Stir in the lemon juice and pepper. Pour over the warm broccoli. Serve immediately.

CARROT-HONEY CASSEROLE

4 carrots, sliced and cooked
1 cup milk
¼ cup butter, melted
3 eggs, beaten
¼ cup honey
2 tablespoons whole wheat flour
1 tablespoon baking powder
¼ teaspoon ground cinnamon
¼ teaspoon ground nutmeg
2 tablespoons toasted wheat germ

Preheat oven to 350°F. Butter a 1-quart ovenproof casserole.

In a food processor or blender, process the carrots and milk until smooth. Add the butter.

In a large bowl, mix the remaining ingredients. Combine with the carrot mixture. Pour into the casserole. Sprinkle wheat germ over the top.

Bake until the mixture is puffed and lightly browned, about 30 minutes.

CRANBERRY-PINEAPPLE SORBET

⅔ cup honey
⅔ cup pineapple juice
4 cups fresh cranberries, pureed
   rind of 1 orange, grated
1 egg white

In a medium-size saucepan, heat the honey and pineapple juice. Stir in the cranberries and orange rind; blend well. Turn the mixture into a shallow metal tray and place in the freezer until partially frozen.

Place mixture in a food processor or blender; process until smooth and fluffy.

Beat the egg white until soft peaks form; fold into the cranberry mixture. Freeze in a covered container.

Remove from the freezer 15 minutes before serving to soften partially.

CURRIED LENTILS

2 tablespoons safflower oil
1 medium-size onion, minced
1 clove garlic, minced
1 tablespoon ground coriander
1 teaspoon curry powder
½ teaspoon ground cumin
½ teaspoon turmeric
   dash of cayenne pepper
2 cups Vegetable Stock (page 35)
   or water
1 medium-size tomato, peeled and
   chopped
1 cup dry lentils
1 tablespoon lemon juice

In a large saucepan or Dutch oven, heat the oil, and sauté the onion until tender. Add the garlic, coriander, curry powder, cumin, turmeric, and cayenne; cook 1 minute.

Add the vegetable stock or water, tomato, and lentils. Cover and simmer until the lentils are tender and the liquid has been absorbed, about 45 minutes. Stir in the lemon juice.

MARINATED HERBED TOMATOES

3 large tomatoes, thinly sliced
⅔ cup safflower oil
¼ cup lemon juice
2 tablespoons chopped fresh parsley
2 scallions, chopped
½ teaspoon dried marjoram
¼ teaspoon pepper
   spinach leaves
3 tablespoons toasted sesame seeds

Place the tomato slices in a shallow pan.

In a small bowl, combine the oil, lemon juice, parsley, scallions, marjoram, and pepper; pour over the tomatoes. Cover and refrigerate overnight.

In a small bowl, combine remaining ingredients. Pour over vegetables and toss. Chill 4 to 6 hours.

MARINATED MIXED VEGETABLES

8 servings

¼ pound green beans, cut into
  1-inch lengths
¼ pound wax beans, cut into 1-inch
  lengths
¼ pound mushrooms, sliced
1 small cucumber, diced
1 stalk celery, cut into ¼-inch slices
1 small green pepper, cut into
  1-inch strips
1 small red onion, chopped
1 medium-size zucchini, cut into
  ¼-inch slices
1 cup cauliflower florets
2 cups cooked chick-peas
½ cup olive or safflower oil
½ cup cider vinegar
1 clove garlic, minced
1 tablespoon lemon juice
1 tablespoon chopped fresh parsley
¼ teaspoon pepper
¼ teaspoon dried chervil
¼ teaspoon dried tarragon
  pinch of cayenne pepper

In a small saucepan, steam green beans and wax beans until crisp-tender. Place in large bowl with mushrooms, cucumber, celery, green pepper, onion, zucchini, cauliflower, and chick-peas; toss gently.

In a small bowl, combine remaining ingredients. Pour over vegetables and toss. Chill 4 to 6 hours.

MEXICAN RICE

2 tablespoons safflower oil
1 cup uncooked brown rice
1 cup chopped tomatoes
2 tablespoons tomato sauce or
    Catsup (page 31)
1 small onion, chopped
2 cloves garlic, minced
2⅓ cups Vegetable Stock (page 35)
1 cup diced carrots, cooked
½ cup peas, cooked
1 tablespoon chopped green chilies
1 tablespoon chopped fresh parsley

Heat the oil in a large saucepan; add the rice and stir until coated with the oil.

In a food processor or blender, process the tomatoes, tomato sauce or catsup, onion, garlic, and ⅓ cup vegetable stock until smooth. Stir into the rice. Add the remaining stock; cover, and cook over medium heat until the liquid has been absorbed and the rice is tender, about 45 minutes.

Stir in the carrots, peas, chilies, and parsley; heat through.

Serve immediately; or, refrigerate for 1 day, and reheat in a saucepan or in an ovenproof casserole at 350°F for 30 minutes.

REFRIED BEANS

2½ cups dry pinto beans
5 cups water
1 medium-size onion, coarsely
    chopped
2 tablespoons butter
2 cloves garlic, minced
1 tablespoon molasses
1 teaspoon chili powder
½ teaspoon pepper

Place the beans in a large saucepan with the water and onion. Bring to a boil, reduce heat, and cook about 1 hour. Drain in a colander, reserving the liquid; set aside.

In the saucepan, heat the butter; add the garlic, and sauté 1 minute. Return beans to the pan; mash with a potato masher, adding some of the reserved bean liquid if necessary. Stir in the molasses, chili powder, and pepper. Cook, stirring, until the beans form a thick puree.

Serve the Refried Beans immediately, or refrigerate for 1 day and reheat in a casserole at 350°F for 30 minutes. The beans are excellent when topped with grated cheddar cheese.

ZUCCHINI PARMESAN

6 servings

    3 tablespoons safflower oil
    6 medium-size zucchini, cut into
        ¼-inch slices
    2 cloves garlic, minced
    4 tablespoons minced onion
    ½ cup grated Parmesan cheese
        (2 ounces)
    1 teaspoon dried oregano
        freshly ground pepper, to taste

Preheat oven to 350°F. Oil a 9×9-inch baking pan.

In a medium-size skillet, heat the oil; add the zucchini, garlic, and onion; sauté until the zucchini is lightly browned, about 5 minutes. Arrange the zucchini in an overlapping pattern in the baking pan.

In a cup, mix the Parmesan, oregano, and pepper. Sprinkle evenly over the zucchini slices. Bake about 25 minutes.

DESSERTS

GLAZED ORANGES

8 servings

    8 large navel oranges
   12 ounces pineapple juice
        concentrate
    4 tablespoons lemon juice

Using a potato peeler, thinly pare the rind from 3 oranges; use a sharp knife to cut the rind into shreds. This procedure may also be done using a zester.

Place the pineapple juice concentrate and the orange rind in a small saucepan. Bring to a rapid boil over medium heat, stirring constantly, until the mixture reduces and darkens slightly, about 5 minutes; do not let it burn. Cool, and stir in lemon juice.

Peel the remaining oranges, removing all the white pith but reserving the rind. Arrange in a flat dish; pour the cooled glaze over the fruit. Garnish with the orange rind, cover, and chill until serving time.

BAKED PEARS WITH LEMON CREAM

6 servings

6 pears, cored
¼ cup honey
¾ cup water
6 whole cloves
Lemon Cream (see following recipe)
freshly ground nutmeg, to taste

Preheat oven to 350°F. Place the pears in a glass baking dish, standing them upright, side by side.

In a medium-size saucepan, bring the honey, water, and cloves to a boil. Pour this mixture over the pears.

Bake until the pears are tender when pierced with a fork, about 30 minutes, depending upon the ripeness of the pears.

Remove the pears from the baking liquid. Serve warm or chilled with Lemon Cream. Top each serving with a grating of nutmeg.

Lemon Cream

Yields 2 cups

1 tablespoon cornstarch
1½ cups milk
1 stick of cinnamon
rind of 2 lemons, grated
¼ cup lemon juice
⅓ cup honey

In a 1-quart saucepan, mix the cornstarch and ¼ cup of the milk; stir until mixture is smooth. Add the remaining milk and the cinnamon. Cook over low heat, stirring constantly, until slightly thick.

Remove pan from heat. Stir in lemon rind, lemon juice, and honey. Remove cinnamon stick, cover, and chill. Pour over warm or chilled Baked Pears just before serving.

LEMON-ORANGE MOUSSE

¼ cup lemon juice
¼ cup orange juice
2 tablespoons cornstarch
5 tablespoons honey
   rind of 1 lemon, grated
   rind of 1 orange, grated
2 eggs, separated
   dash of cream of tartar
1 cup heavy cream
½ teaspoon vanilla extract
1 lemon, sliced, or 6 strawberries

In a small saucepan, mix the lemon juice, orange juice, cornstarch, 4 tablespoons of the honey, lemon rind, and orange rind. When the mixture is smooth, cook over low heat until it starts to thicken, 5 to 7 minutes. Remove from heat.

Lightly beat the egg yolks. Stir 2 tablespoons of the warm juice mixture into the yolks; then add to the mixture in the saucepan. Beat until smooth. Refrigerate.

When the juice-egg yolk mixture has chilled and started to gel, about 30 minutes, beat the egg whites with the cream of tartar until they form stiff peaks. Fold into the chilled juice mixture.

Beat the cream until thick; beat in the remaining honey and the vanilla. Set aside ¼ of this mixture for garnish; chill. Fold the remainder into the mousse.

Divide among 4 to 6 small dessert cups or pour into one large serving bowl; chill several hours before serving.

Garnish each serving with a dollop of the sweetened whipped cream. Top with a lemon slice or a fresh strawberry.

MANGO CREAM

3 large mangoes
1 orange, cubed
1 tablespoon lemon juice
1 cup heavy cream
1 tablespoon honey
½ cup finely chopped pecans

Peel the mangoes; place in a food processor or blender, process until smooth. Stir in the orange and the lemon juice.

Beat the cream; when peaks form, whip in the honey. Fold into the mango mixture. Chill.

Spoon into dessert dishes; top each serving with chopped pecans.

PUMPKIN CUSTARD

2 tablespoons butter
4 eggs
5 tablespoons honey
3 cups hot milk
1⅓ cups cooked pumpkin, mashed
2 teaspoons grated lemon rind
fresh nutmeg

Preheat oven to 325°F. Butter 10 custard cups; place in a large baking pan.

In a large bowl, beat the eggs; add the honey. Slowly add the milk, continuing to beat. Then beat in the pumpkin and lemon rind; mix thoroughly.

Divide among the custard cups; grate nutmeg on top of each. Pour hot water into the pan around the custard cups. Bake until a knife inserted in the center comes out clean, about 30 minutes.

The custard is tasty when served at room temperature or chilled.

For variety, other raw or dried fruits, alone or in combination, can be substituted for the pumpkin. If dried fruit is used, soak it in warm water until it is soft; drain well before mashing.

Index

avocados *(continued)*
    Avocado-Sprout Salad, 119
    Guacamole, 178
    Spinach-Avocado Salad, 123

B

Baked Apples in Orange Sauce, 134
Baked Bananas with Raisin-Walnut Sauce, 135
Baked Chili Rellenos, 194
Baked Pears with Lemon Cream, 200
Baked Sauced Mushrooms, 52
bananas
    Baked Bananas with Raisin-Walnut Sauce, 135
    Banana-Apricot Bread, 57
    Banana Frozen Yogurt, 135
    Banana-Pecan Butter, 29
    Banana-Wheat Germ Muffins, 86
    Granola Banana Splits, 45
basics
    Apple Butter, 29
    Apricot-Apple Spread, 32
    Banana-Pecan Butter, 29
    butters, 29-30
    Catsup, 31
    Cinnamon-Honey Butter, 30
    condiments, 31-32
    fruit butters, 29
    Granola, 27, 33
    Herb Butter, 30
    Honey Butter, 30
    Lecithin Mixture, 33
    Lemon-Honey Butter, 29
    Maple Butter, 30
    Mayonnaise, 31
    Mustard, 31
    Orange Honey, 32
    Orange-Honey Butter, 29
    Orange-Pineapple Butter, 29
    preparation of basics, 7
    Quick Herb-Cheese Spread, 32
    Ricotta-Orange Spread, 32
    Safflower Butter, 30
    Seasoned Whole Wheat Croutons, 27, 34
    spreads, 32-33
    Strawberry-Honey Butter, 29
    sweetened butters, 30
    Tangerine Cream Cheese, 33
    Tomato Hot Sauce, 34
    use of basics, 7, 27
    Vegetable Stock, 35
bean curd, *see* tofu
beans, *see* chick-peas, dried beans, green
        beans, kidney beans, lentils, mung beans,
        pinto beans
Bean Sprout-Apple Salad, 119
bean sprouts, *see* mung beans
bean thread, *see Harusame* noodles

Bechamel Sauce, 69
beverages
    Cranberry Special, 42
    Fruit Blend Supreme, 42
    Hot Apple Tea, 42
    Hot Spiced Cider, 43
    Hot Spiced Pineapple Juice, 43
    Hot Spiced Tomato Juice, 43
    Morning Punch, 44
    Orange Juliet, 44
    Strawberry Frappé, 44
    Warming Grape-Cinnamon Punch, 44
biscuits, *see* breads
black mushrooms, dried, description of, 16-17
Blintzes, Whole Wheat-Cheese, 54
bran
    Apple-Raisin Bran Muffins, 130
    description of, 14
    Maple-Orange Bran Muffins, 89
    Orange Bran Muffins, 60
breads
    Apple-Raisin Bran Muffins, 130
    Apricot Muffins, 86
    Banana-Apricot Bread, 57
    Banana-Wheat Germ Muffins, 86
    Buttermilk-Whole Wheat Quick Bread, 87
    Carrot Corn Muffins, 58
    Cheese Sticks, 176
    Cracked Wheat Bread, 87
    Crusty Rye Bread, 58
    Date and Wheat Germ Muffins, 88
    Flaky Brown Rice Biscuits, 111
    Granola Bars, 59
    Herbed Biscuits, 88
    Herbed Muffins, 162
    Honey-Pumpkin Muffins, 89
    Irish Soda Bread, 59
    Many-Grain Maple Muffins, 162
    Maple-Orange Bran Muffins, 89
    Mixed Grain-Honey Corn Bread, 131
    Molasses-Rye Muffins, 132
    Orange Bran Muffins, 60
    Peanut Butter-Oatmeal Muffins, 60
    Pineapple-Pecan Muffins, 61
    Quick Bread Sticks, 90
    Rye Biscuits, 131
    Spicy Carrot Muffins, 90
    Tofu Bread Sticks, 91
    Whole Wheat Crescent Rolls, 163
    Whole Wheat French Bread, 181
    Whole Wheat-Orange Toast, 132
Brie, Pecan-Topped, 85
broccoli
    Broccoli-Almond Soufflé Roll, 46
    Broccoli in Lemon Butter and Pine Nuts, 194
    Cauli-Broc Quiche, 146
    Cheesy Broccoli Shortcake, 111

cheese *(continued)*
  Vegetable-Cheese Nachos, 179
  Vegetable-Cheese Strata, 52
  Walnut-Cheese Nuggets, 127
  Whole Wheat-Cheese Blintzes, 54
  Zucchini-Ricotta Casserole, 75
Cheesecake, Nut-Crusted Ricotta, 97
Chef's Salad, Vegetarian, 73
chick-peas (garbanzo beans)
  description of, 16
  Hummus, 177
Chili, Cashew, 110
Chili Rellenos, Baked, 194
Chili Sauce, Sweet-and-Hot, 183
Chilled Cucumber Soup, 80
Chilled Orange-Yogurt Soup, 81
Chinese Vegetable Salad, 66
Chinese Watercress Soup, 156
Chinese yam, *see* jicama
Cider, Hot Spiced, 43
Cinnamon-Honey Butter, 30
coconut
  Coconut-Honey Date Bars, 93
  Honey-Coconut Crust, 164
  Pineapple-Coconut Sherbet, 168
Concasse of Tomato, 81
condiments
  Catsup, 31
  Mayonnaise, 31
  Mustard, 31
  Orange Honey, 32
cookies
  Carob Chip Cookies, 91
  Whole Wheat-Almond Cookies, 171
corn
  Carrot Corn Muffins, 58
  corn oil, description of, 21
  Kidney Bean-Corn Pie, 113
  Mixed Grain-Honey Corn Bread, 131
Cottage Cheese Sauce, 69
couscous, description of, 15
Couscous with Vegetable-Cashew Sauce and
    Parsley-Egg Sauce, 66-67
cracked wheat, description of, 14, 15
Cracked Wheat Bread, 87
cranberries
  Cranberry Applesauce, 54
  Cranberry-Pineapple Sorbet, 195
  Cranberry Special, 42
Cream Cheese, Tangerine, 33
Cream of Green-Pea Carrot Soup, 82
Cream of Mushroom Soup, 193
Creamy Basil Dressing, 74
Creamy French Dressing, 77
Creamy Garlic Dressing, 122
Creamy Herb Dressing, 125
Creamy Tomato Vegetable Soup, 126

crepes
  Garden Vegetable Crepes, 148
  Gateau des Crepes, 68-69
  Wheat Germ Crepes, 148
  Whole Wheat Crepes, 68
Croutons, Seasoned Whole Wheat, 27, 34
Crusty Rye Bread, 58
cucumbers
  Chilled Cucumber Soup, 80
  Cucumber-Carrot Salad, 120
  Cucumber-Yogurt Salad, 76
  Cumin Cucumber Salad, 120
Cumin Cucumber Salad, 120
Curried Lentils, 196
Curried Tomato-Rice Salad, 120
Curry, Calcutta, 182
custard
  Fresh Peach Custard Pie, 94
  Honey-Vanilla Custard, 101
  Pumpkin Custard, 202

D

dates
  Coconut-Honey Date Bars, 93
  Date and Wheat Germ Muffins, 88
desserts
  Apple Crisp, 133
  Apricot Whip, 133
  Baked Apples in Orange Sauce, 134
  Baked Bananas with Rasin-Walnut Sauce, 135
  Baked Pears with Lemon Cream, 200
  Banana Frozen Yogurt, 135
  Carob Chiffon Pie, 164
  Carob Chip Cookies, 91
  Carob Creme Patisserie, 134
  Carob-Dipped Strawberries, 93
  Carob-Honey Brownies, 92
  Carob-Pecan Torte, 165
  Carob-Pineapple Cream, 136
  Coconut-Honey Date Bars, 93
  French Apple Tart, 166
  Fresh Fruit Custard Pie, 94
  Fresh Fruit Fondue, 137
  Frozen Apricot-Orange Mousse, 137
  Fruit Platter Pie, 95
  Glazed Oranges, 199
  Honey-Carrot Cake, 138
  Honey-Lemon Chiffon Pie, 167
  Honey-Pumpkin Mousse, 136
  Honey-Rice Pudding, 96
  Honey-Spiced Pound Cake, 169
  Honey-Vanilla Creme Patisserie, 169
  Honey-Vanilla Custard, 101
  Kiwi Sherbet, 96
  Lemon-Orange Mousse, 201
  Mango Cream, 202
  Maple-Sauced Oranges, 139

W

walnuts
  Carrot-Nut Loaf, 109
  Raisin-Walnut Sauce, 135
  Walnut-Cheese Nuggets, 127
  Walnut Torte, 102
  Walnut Vegetable Salad, 79
  Walnut-Wild Rice Pilaf, 130
Warming Grape-Cinnamon Punch, 44
Watercress Soup, Chinese, 156
wheat, *see also* wheat germ, whole wheat
  cracked wheat, description of, 14, 15
  Cracked Wheat Bread, 87
wheat germ
  Banana-Wheat Germ Muffins, 86
  Date and Wheat Germ Muffins, 88
  description of, 24
  Oatmeal-Wheat Germ Crust, 94
  Wheat Germ Crepes, 148
  Wheat Germ Fried Noodles, 85
White Grape Mousse, 103
Whole Grain Hot Cereal, 53
whole wheat
  Buttermilk-Whole Wheat Quick Bread, 87
  Whole Wheat-Almond Cookies, 171
  Whole Wheat-Cheese Blintzes, 54
  Whole Wheat Cookie Crust, 95
  Whole Wheat Crepes, 68
  Whole Wheat Crescent Rolls, 163
  whole wheat flour, description of, 17
  Whole Wheat French Bread, 181

whole wheat *(continued)*
  Whole Wheat-Orange Toast, 132
  Whole Wheat Pastry, 100
  whole wheat pastry flour, description of, 17
  whole wheat pita bread pockets, 71, 72
  Whole Wheat Puffs, 170
  Whole Wheat-Sesame Crust, 146
  Whole Wheat Spaghetti with Nutballs in
    Marinara Sauce, 188-189
wild rice, description of, 24
Winter Salad, 153

Y

yogurt
  Apricot-Yogurt Dressing, 151
  Banana Frozen Yogurt, 135
  Chilled Orange-Yogurt Soup, 81
  Cucumber-Yogurt Salad, 76
  description of, 24-25
  Fresh Tomato-Yogurt Soup, 83
  Maple-Yogurt Gingerbread, 139
  Stewed Fruit and Yogurt, 57
  Vanilla Yogurt, 51
  Yogurt Hollandaise, 48

Z

zucchini
  Zucchini Parmesan, 199
  Zucchini-Ricotta Casserole, 75
  Zucchini Soup, 157
  Zucchini Stuffed with Lentils and Tomatoes, 118